Prevention in Mental Health

Prevention in Mental Health

edited by
Henri Parens and
Selma Kramer

JASON ARONSON INC.
Northvale, New Jersey
London

This book is set in 11.5 pt. Bem by Lind Graphics of Upper Saddle River, New Jersey, and printed and bound by Haddon Craftsmen of Scranton, Pennsylvania.

10 9 8 7 6 5 4 3 2 1

Library of Congress Cataloging-in-Publication Data

Prevention in mental health / edited by Henri Parens and Selma Kramer.
p. cm.
Includes bibliographical references and index.
ISBN 1-56821-027-2 (pbk.)
1. Child mental health. 2. Parental influences. 3. Mental illness—Prevention. 4. Mental health promotion. 5. Parenting—Study and teaching. I. Parens, Henri, 1928– . II. Kramer, Selma.
[DNLM: 1. Affective Disorders—prevention & control—congresses. 2. Affective Disorders—in infancy & childhood—congresses. 3. Parenting—congresses. 4. Parents—education—congresses. WS 350.6 P944 1993]
RJ507.P35P74 1993
618.92'8905—dc20
DNLM/DLC
for Libary of Congress 93-19429

Manufactured in the United States of America. Jason Aronson Inc. offers books and cassettes. For information and catalog write to Jason Aronson Inc., 230 Livingston Street, Northvale, New Jersey 07647.

CONTENTS

PREFACE

This volume grows out of the 23rd Annual Margaret S. Mahler Child Development Symposium "Prevention in Mental Health: Today, Tomorrow, Ever?" held in Philadelphia on May 16, 1992. Although the idea of prevention is a constant in the annual Margaret S. Mahler Symposium, this was the first specifically committed to the question of prevention in mental health. Each Symposium presenter and each discussant was given the opportunity to enlarge his/her time-limited presentation to a full-length book chapter. The chapter by Frank and Rowe, the opening chapter by Parens, and the closing chapter by Kramer were added. The Philadelphia Symposium, in a modified form, was also held in the Durham-Chapel Hill area, on October 31, 1992.

1

A CALL FOR PREVENTION

Henri Parens, M.D.

The work presented in this volume affirms and is based on the conviction held by its contributors that we can and must make greater efforts than we have to date toward preventing the development of *experience-derived* emotional disorders. We do not address the prevention of inborn diatheses that determine or predispose to mental illness (e.g., primary autism or genetic factors in bipolar illness); our science does not have this capability. But the conviction is large among psychodynamic clinicians and researchers that the many experential factors that activate or facilitate the development of mental illness, especially neglect, physical and sexual abuse, and traumatizing child rearing, can be mitigated and/or modified. In addition, some of the contributors call for a significant increase in our efforts to develop strategies for early intervention (and therewith secondary prevention) in large groups of children already at risk for serious maladaptation and mental ill-health.

The politics of psychiatry is known to us all and, as in human thought and science throughout the history of civilization, has brought reciprocal denunciations and outrageous falsifications among rival schools. But it has also wrought wondrous progress. Just as Mark Twain observed that reports of his demise were premature and predictions of the demise of the American family absolutely improbable, so too are the death knoll soundings for psychoanalysis and dynamic psychotherapies—heard in some corners of our land—misinformed, premature, and improbable. From these corners comes the disclaimer that early childhood experiences are not determining of later development (Kagan 1984) nor of personality altogether (Bridger 1989). In Chapter 6 I shall argue this disclaimer in order to underscore the merits of the work presented by the contributors of this volume. Were the claim to prove correct that childhood experiences do not contribute to the determination of personality, mental health, and adaptation, the contents of this volume would be meaningless. If, however, as I shall detail in Chapter 6, this hypothesis can be rejected, then the contents of this volume warrant wide dissemination among institutions concerned with the mental health of children and adults.

Evidence coming from neurobiology (Cunningham 1992, Kandel et al. 1991, Post 1992)—which would have been a source of much excitement for neurobiologist Freud—as well as from biogenetics (Ginsburg 1982), immunology (Calabrese et al. 1987), and neuropsychology (e.g., on the influence of experience on renewed brain function in stroke victims and on the plasticity of the brain [Cunningham 1992, Rourke and colleagues 1983]) give validity to the hypothesis that experience is codeterminer with inborn biogenetic dispositions of *somatic* structure formation and function. This evidence gives validity not only to continuity theory, but also the *the genetic point of view* of psychoanalysis, which holds that early life experiences impact on the child's inborn dispositions to progressively organize patterns of adaptation (Sander 1985) and psychic structure formation. Furthermore, this patterning and structure formation achieve stability—while retaining a relative plasticity—as the child continues to mature and develop (Hartmann 1950). The fact that experience continues to impact on the child in the course of development allows for the plausible assumptions of discontinuity theory without invalidating our assuming existing continuities, a seeming paradox to some. This seeming paradox, which is in fact a complementarity, is contained in all psychoanalytic developmental theories currently available to us including psychosexual theory (Abraham 1924, Freud 1905), psychosocial theory (Erikson 1959), adaptive child–mother interaction theory (Sander 1962, Sander et al. 1979), separation-individuation theory (Mahler 1965, Mahler et al. 1975), epigenesis of aggression theory (Parens 1979a, 1989b), and developmental structuralist theory (Greenspan 1981, 1989).

In this volume, the contributors are speaking of the prevention of *experience-derived* emotional disorders and maladaptations as well as of early intervention with children already at risk for mental ill-health and maladaptation. What many of us feel must be done is to develop strategies for the prevention of what untoward pathogenetic experiences bring to that which is inborn. Many of those committed to such work see optimizing parenting as the widest avenue to prevention. And as my collaborators and I have found, child rearing spans a wide range from growth-promoting to growth-disturbing parenting (Parens et al. 1986b, Parens et al. 1987, Parens et al. 1989). We find that influencing parenting in at-risk families so as to shift their child rearing toward the growth-promoting range is achievable (Parens et al. 1993a), and we assume that it leads to child rearing that at least facilitates, and perhaps may even optimize, the child's inborn capacities for healthy emotional life and adaptation.

Much new knowledge from the varied mental health disciplines has led to a number of valuable contributions that can aid in developing strategies for the prevention of experience-derived emotional disorders (Ainsworth et al. 1978, Fraiberg 1980, Greenspan 1992, Greenspan and Greenspan 1985, Parens et al. 1987, 1993a, Provence and Naylor 1983). This is attested to by the contributors to this volume. The plea of this volume was well stated by Bowlby, who noted with regard to the rich and promising implications that attachment research is showing:

> If, by exploiting this new knowledge the burden of mental ill health is to be reduced, western societies will have to give far more attention to measures that encourage and support stable family life than any do at present. What the social, economic, and political implications of such measures might be, if they are to be effective, will require very serious study and may well be far reaching. Experts from many fields will be required. Yet substantial progress in this important area cannot be expected until members of the mental health professions speak with a more united voice then they do at present. [1989, pp. 264–265]

Without more involvement by mental health professionals we believe current efforts will fall too short of their goals. Although as always there are voices of dissent, this volume attests that there are mental health professionals involved in just such efforts. Our plea is based on the conviction that the state of our knowledge, although limited, is nonetheless sufficient to allow a meaningful penetration into the realm of prevention. In fact, social conditions defy the time needed for more solid proof. Some of the proof will have to come from the prevention efforts being researched for their effectiveness. In this spirit, the principal presenters of this volume put before us the prevention work and programs each has developed.

CONTENTS OF THIS VOLUME

Byron Egeland and Martha Erickson open their chapter with a brief description of attachment theory, its basic assumptions, and classification of attachment patterns. Egeland and Erickson note that a number of prevention programs specifically aimed at preventing parenting dysfunctions and child maladaption have been developed and carried out. A variety of models exist, from public health models to mental health, parent education, and social support models. They wonder if the mixed results attained by home visitation programs derive from the intervention having focused on the child or the parent "with little emphasis on the relationship" (p. 23).

They describe their STEEP Program (Steps Toward Effective Enjoyable Parenting), which is in part modeled on Fraiberg's (1980) homebound "therapy in the kitchen." A key goal is their attempt to modify the mothers' inner working models (IWMs) by attempting to have mothers face their own developmental history, examine how it affects their parenting, express the pain associated with their past and present, look at parent choices and actions, and consider how they can feel more empowered. STEEP is a one year program, starting prior to the infants' birth, consisting of home visitations and mother–child groups. The authors discuss their findings. They recognize that while they are disappointed in their attachment classification results, they recognize that some of their positive findings are strong and may later prove to have positively impacted on the mother–child relationship and therewith on the child's attachment, development, and adaptation.

The authors assert that whatever model—be it based on the development of intelligence schemas, internal representations of psychoanalytic theory, Bowlby's "internal working models," or neurobiological epigenetic concepts—there is agreement that personality formation becomes progressively structured from the earliest months of life on and, therefore, prevention programs would do well to aim at optimizing parenting from infancy on.

Patricia Nachman, discussing Egeland's and Erickson's STEEP program, draws attention to the power and usefulness of attachment theory and its foremost research instrument, the Ainsworth Strange Situation. She notes their limitations—which are expectable with any theory or measure addressing just one, however major, parameter of the child's psychic life—in explaining the totality of psychic functioning we look for in psychic experiencing and in the clinical situation. Nonetheless, like Nachman, I believe attachment theory, as a modest variant of the psychoanalytic models of the developmental and qualitative features of the child's constructing a psychic relationship to primary objects,[1] addresses one of the most fundamental determiners of psychic structure formation, mental health, and adaptation. Freud's 1923 hypothesis that the development of the ego and the superego are the precipitates of the history of the child's object relations bespeaks the long existing recognition by psychoanalysis of the centrality of the libidinal objects to the child's psychic structure formation. And although there are limitations to the Ainsworth Strange Situation, the original measure being applicable only to the twelve to eighteen months period (recent efforts have yielded measures for later developmental periods as well), we are looking at a near-critical period for attachment, a period during which the basic elements of emotional relatedness, libidinal cathexis (or attachment), achieve a first level of psychic structuralization.

In this sense then, attachment theory and the Ainsworth Strange Situation are powerful constructs that can evaluate an aspect of psychic functioning critical to the total development and adaptation of the child and, as has been shown (Sroufe 1982), has some predictive capabilities with regard to adaptation and

1. The other powerfully developed theories are Spitz's (1965) Structuring of the Libidinal Object and Mahler's (1965, Mahler et al., 1975) Separation-Individuation Theory. I say modest because the foremost difference between Bowlby's model and those of Spitz and Mahler (Bowlby's genetic postulate being ethologically based and that of Spitz and Mahler being libido theory and ego psychologically based) are of modest consequence to the clinical and research applications of the development of the child's emotional relationship to the mother (or other constant enough primary caregiver).

mental health. These are valuable constructs, Nachman believes, that serve psychoanalysis equally well as developmental psychology, and are invaluable contributions to both fields. Furthermore, Nachman credits—as do I—Ainsworth for having operationalized Bowlby's scientific framework, a feat that has been difficult to achieve in psychoanalysis, one that bridges and fosters a most welcome rapprochement between psychoanalysis and developmental psychology. As Nachman emphasizes, the more recent move beyond attachment theory's ethological beginnings toward the more subjective aspect of attachment is yet another step in this rapprochement.

In her very cogent discussion of Egeland and Erickson's paper, Nachman draws attention to the overly optimistic assumption made by Egeland and Erickson that significant changes in IWMs of their at-risk young mothers could be effected over the course of only one year of interventions by means of twice monthly home visits and twice monthly mothers' group developmental guidance (Fraiberg 1980). Our own Prevention/Early Intervention Mother–Child Groups required at least 18 months of twice *weekly* developmental guidance (Parens 1988) before we began to see a sufficient change in parenting functions effecting a shift from growth-disturbing to growth-promoting rearing (Parens, this volume, Chapter 7).

Furthermore, Nachman also points to the object loss factor and the possibility of its disorganizing potential, which may have occurred at the end of the one year program when some of the young mothers probably had become attached to the program staff who were now no longer available to them. But while Egeland and Erickson were disappointed in their attachment classification findings, Nachman tells them that perhaps they are insufficiently highlighting the positive changes they found in the STEEP mothers as compared to the control mothers, changes Egeland and Erickson recognize to be of documented importance to growth-promoting parenting.

From the outset of her chapter, Eleanor Galenson decries

the "grave shortage of mental health professionals trained to carry out appropriate treatment programs [for] the vast number of emotionally disturbed and developmentally delayed very young children . . . in this country" (p. 63). "More training programs will have to be established," she asserts, and these should preferrably be "under the aegis of mental health academic institutions" (p. 63).

The uniqueness of her presentation is that Galenson reports on her 1980 decade of clinical experience with at-risk infants from both clinic-based low-income and private practice-based upper-income infants and their parents. She reports on her private practice work with forty-five children under 3 years of age when first seen, treated jointly with their parents, and on sixty-five clinic-based child-mother pairs who, out of 165 whom she evaluated, remained in their treatment program for one to three years.

Galenson speaks of this clinic population, but not of her private practice population, as being "at *high* risk" (italics added). For the high risk infants, they provided each mother-child pair three two-hour treatment sessions per week, one-on-one with a psychotherapist. In addition, a mothers group and home visitations were provided. Galenson reports in detail on her findings, and notes that environmental factors seem overwhelmingly determining stressors, and in her treatment approach she attempts to address the wider environmental influences that impact on these mother-child pairs.

Thinking in terms of secondary prevention, Galenson feels that "more trained mental health professionals are a prime requirement if we are to mount a successful program for *treating* this vast group of very young but already deviant children" (p. 81, italics added). It is her impression that modifications of therapeutic approaches, which she discusses, will be necessary to be effective. She opts for "a full-day therapeutic experience in which the young child spends the greater part of his early years within a structured program carried out under the supervision of trained mental health professionals" (p. 82). At the same time, she suggests that the mother should have the opportunity for therapeutic treatment appropriate to her own needs. She believes such a program should be tested. Galenson concludes with the thought that the time has come for us "to face the unpleasant reality that none of our therapeutic models has as yet proven sufficiently effective in the early intervention . . . of the psychological disorders of the seriously at-risk infants from this economically and socially deprived segment of our population" (p. 82).

In the course of discussing Galenson's presentation, J. Alexis Burland reports on his experiences in a program that attempted a variety of innovative therapeutic approaches. He cautions against idealism, which closes our eyes to the large degree of difficulty inherent in changing the traumatizing rearing he observed in the most dysfunctional mothers in their high-risk group. Reared by parents with past histories of having themselves been severely abused and traumatized, the children he worked with showed significant problems in development and adaptation.

Burland incisively calls us all to task for assuming over-optimistically, if not naively, that nature itself will ensure that parents will provide the environment children need to form secure attachments, that more and more demonstrated necessary foundation for healthy emotional development. He justifiably asks of health professionals why child rearing is so neglected in our science, a question that profiled itself highly in his efforts to help severely dysfunctional parents. He also fears the naive optimism that does not recognize the need for adequate training for intervenors, the sweeping changes and multiple approaches required to rehabilitate dysfunctional families, and the cost of time, energy, and money required to provide effective help.

Burland notes the fact that we should not speak of prevention when we work with highly dysfunctional families. Much therapeutic work is needed with dysfunctional parents and early therapeutic intervention is needed with their young children. Burland believes that therapeutic programs for dysfunctional families—perhaps the kind proposed by Galenson—should be the first level of effort, and that secondary prevention will follow to the degree that the therapeutic efforts succeed.

It is exactly to this point, to the serious problems and the major dilemma we professionals and society face, that William M. Singletary and I address ourselves. My collaborators and I feel (see Chapter 7, this volume) that we cannot address only the present enormous problems that need our attention; we must think long term as well. In addition to the treatment programs called for by Galenson and Burland, and to intervention programs like that of Egeland and Erickson, we must look to ways to prevent the next generation of children from meeting the same painful fate as have their parents. We do not want the next generation of 13-year-olds to suffer the same chaos as many of today's 13-year-olds, nor do we want them to require the enormous amounts of government money and society funding as do so many of today's youths. The price of not thinking ahead is far greater than that of doing so.

In Chapter 6 I present findings from neurobiology in support of the genetic point of view of psychoanalysis and in support of the prevention and early intervention efforts made by this volume's contributors. I take note of our own longitudinal observational findings and those of McDevitt (1991) that patterns of reactivity and adaptation persist from early life to later years. It is in these patterns that Sander (1985) believes continuity of early development into later adaptation shows itself. This is contrary to the propositions put forth by discontinuity theorists (Kagan 1984) and by biological psychiatrists who select epidemiological studies to attempt to disprove the hypothesis that childhood experiences (especially in human relationships) influence the development of personality (Bridger 1989).

The argument I present is based on the biogenetic theory that experience is a central contributor to the specific phenotype yielded by a given genotype. I then present a series of findings from biological disciplines including long known findings in neuro-ophthomology (that lack of eye function leads to neuronal and optic nerve atrophy), more recent findings in immunology (that stress lowers immunologic responsiveness), in brain trauma and medical therapeutic intervention (that function loss in stroke victims can be reacquired by nondamaged or possibly regenerated brain tissue following training of the patients), in brain anatomical research (that experience impacts on interconnectivity of brain cells), and I detail some of the more recent findings from neurobiology, that is, the work of Kandel and colleagues (1991) on the influence of experience on synaptic modulation and synapse formation, and that of R. M. Post (1992) on the influence of stress (experience) on the stimulation of biogenetic factors that activate gene expression.

I also take note of the empirical findings of Harlow (1960, Harlow and Harlow 1962) on rhesus monkeys isolated during childhood and on the influence of this highly traumatizing experience on their brains and behaviors, work replicated and continued by Suomi (1982, 1991).

These data document more and more determinedly that experience and biogenetic dispositions codetermine personality, mental health, and adaptation.

I start Chapter 7, "Toward the Prevention of Experience-Derived Emotional Disorders by Education for Parenting," with a clarion call for the engagement of mental health professionals in the prevention of experience-derived emotional disorders. In order to cogently present the prevention work in which our group is engaged, I have briefly traced the history of the steps by which we arrived at our decision to push for the institution, in primary and secondary schools, of psychodynamically informed curriculums on education for mental health-promoting parenting.

I briefly note the beginnings of this group's work—the original group including Elizabeth Scattergood, Robert C. Prall, Leafy Pollock, Peter Bennett, Andrina Duff, Rogelio Hernit, and others—which evolved from attempts to correlate qualitative aspects of the mother–child relationship with the development of specific ego functions in the child, into the recognition that we had adventitiously found a method for teaching growth-promoting parenting to the parents in our first mother–child group; we labeled this method "Prevention/Early Intervention Mother-Child Groups" (Parens 1988, Parens et al. 1974). I briefly describe this method. At the same time, further adventitious findings led us to study the development of aggression in early childhood and to a reformation of the psychoanalytic theory of aggression (Parens 1973, 1979a,b, 1989a,b). A central hypothesis yielded from this work, that "Excessive Unpleasure experiences instigate the generation of Hostile Destructiveness," opened to view a remarkable possibility that we organized into the project, "Toward Preventing the Development of Excessive Hostility in Children" (Parens et al. 1982, Parens et al. 1986a, Parens et al. 1987). As we progressed in our efforts toward preventing the development of excessive hostility, we also began to develop a curriculum for teaching parenting to students in grades K through 12. The text of this curriculum is currently in a first draft. To give the reader an idea of the structure and content of the curriculum, a brief description is presented in Chapter 7. The feasibility of teaching parenting to school-age children was amply demonstrated by the teachers of a local private school with whom we worked for a number of years. Thanks to their work with us, the teachers developed their own introductory curriculum, *Learning About Parenting* (Heath et al. 1983), which they have been teaching for over ten years now in a number of cities including Philadelphia, New York, and Chicago. Out of interest in follow-up studies and in an attempt to demonstrate the effectiveness of open-ended participation in a Prevention/Early Intervention Parent-Child Group, we began the process of evaluating and reporting on the nineteen-year follow-up study of our first group participants, children and their mothers. In Chapter 7 we present some preliminary results (Parens et al. 1993a); the study is ongoing.

I then conclude Chapter 7 with a description of our current collaboration efforts with the teachers and administrators of Education For Parenting (the group with whom we have worked for a number of years), our Parenting Education Middle School Initiative, an educational parenting curriculum for all students in grades six through eight in a specific Philadelphia public school, as well as a comprehensive parenting program for those sixth to eighth graders in that school who already are mothers. We also outline our research strategy for phase two of this project.

William M. Singletary surveyed a group of prevention studies and echoes Schorr (1988) and Hamburg (1992) in the feasibility of prevention. Singletary takes note of Margaret Mahler's conviction that education of parents would serve prevention and early intervention. He reviews education for parenting programs including Burton White's New Parents as Teachers and Rauh and colleagues' Mother–Infant Transaction Program, to highlight that such well-conducted programs are significantly improving parenting and child emotional and adaptive development. He then briefly reviews several comprehensive prevention programs including the Perry Preschool Program, the Yale Child Welfare Program directed by Sally Provence, the Prenatal/Early Infant Project directed by David Olds, and the Hawaii Healthy Start program. Singletary argues that despite the difficulties inherent in evaluating the cost effectiveness of such programs, measurable (e.g., actual dollars) and nonmeasurable (e.g., quality of life) parameters of such evaluation indicate their noteworthy cost effectiveness. In accord with the duly hailed 1988 report by Lisbeth Schorr, *Within Our Reach,* Singletary concludes with conviction that a number of comprehensive prevention and early intervention programs have proven to be affordable and cost-effective.

John B. McDevitt endorses the views and concerns expressed by Singletary and me. To my assertion that "Prevention is not in the minds of most mental health professionals," he feels this to be unfortunate since a number of epidemiological studies have identified important risk factors in childhood psychiatric, cognitive, and social disorders. This is furthermore so, McDevitt adds, since as Singletary reports, prevention does work and is cost effective. Borrowing on the adage that an ounce of prevention is worth a pound of cure, McDevitt points out that "there is no satisfactory solution to these disorders since . . . we do not have the ability or the resources to provide effective treatment once they have become established" (Chapter 9, p. 169). McDevitt puts this dilemma in a larger social context, quoting Galbraith, who asserts that the contented majority has turned its back on the underclass, on those who are disadvantaged and at risk. McDevitt draws attention to the burden new prevention efforts sustain in having to compete for very limited funds with programs such as Headstart that have already been shown to work and to be cost effective. In contrast to the acceptance of certain medical health promotion and prevention programs, prevention in the mental health field is not easily understood, proven or shown to be effective and is much more expensive. Despite these difficulties inherent in mental health prevention research, and those facing Parens, Singletary, and their collaborators, McDevitt, himself a renowned long-time researcher and clinician, thinks that the effort will prove to be worthwile and that the short-term and long-term predictions will be supported.

Considering one of Nachman's criticisms of the STEEP project, Galenson and Burland's concern for more intensive and mental health trained interventional efforts, and my own report of the time and frequency of intervention needed to effect a change toward growth-promoting parenting, McDevitt affirms that Mahler and Fraiberg also emphasized the need for frequent and long-term educational and therapeutic efforts to effect a beneficial prevention and early interventional result.

In their chapter, Elaine Frank and Denise Rowe report on their decade of experience training professionals in a parenting education method and their nearly twenty years of applying this education for parenting method in a wide variety of settings (hospitals, schools) and contexts (abusive parents, foster parents, adoptive parents). They briefly describe the training program developed by Rogelio Hernit and Parens, which they taught to health professionals, a program that trains health professionals to carry out the Prevention/Early Intervention Parent–Child Groups method developed by Parens and colleagues (Parens 1988, Parens et al. 1974). They also tell us of the awakening recognition in the community of the need for parenting education services in a number of settings. Their particular interest in and work with adoptive parents makes a unique contribution to a much neglected subset of parents who experience specific problems as well as the usual taxing ones experienced by all devoted parents. Their narrative only hints at the low cost of the wide and widening scope of the services they continue to render.

Selma Kramer, a dean of American Child Psychoanalysis and Psychiatry as well as organizer and coordinator of the past twenty-three Annual Margaret S. Mahler Child Development Symposia, closes this book with crucial questions. Where does prevention in mental health fit in society, in the changing family structure, and in government? Dr. Kramer sees wider scope and narrower scope domains of activities that need to be mobilized to secure a better, healthier, and safer life for our children, and therewith of society. Dr. Kramer feels that in order to be successful, a massive collaboration is essential between health sciences and a host of organizations.

REFERENCES

Abraham, K. (1924). A short study of the development of libido. In *Selected Papers of Karl Abraham,* pp. 418–501. New York: Basic Books, 1953.

Ainsworth, M., Blehar, M., Waters, E., and Walls, S. (1978). *Patterns of Attachment.* Hillsdale, NJ: Lawrence Erlbaum.

Bowlby, J. (1989). The role of attachment in personality development and psychopathology. In *The Course of Life.* Vol. I: *Infancy,* ed. S. I. Greenspan and G. H. Pollock, pp. 229–270. Madison, CT: International Universities Press.

Bridger, W. (1989). Child rearing and personality development: fact and fiction. Presidential address to the Society of Biological Psychiatry, May 4, San Francisco.

Calabrese, J. R., Kling, M. A., and Gold, P. W. (1987). Alterations in immunocompetence during stress, bereavement, and depression: focus on neuroendocrine regulation. *American Journal of Psychiatry* 144:1123–1134.

Cunningham, T. (1992). Personal communication.

Erikson, E. H. (1959). Identity and the life cycle. *Psychological Issues,* Monogr. 1. New York: International Universities Press.

Fraiberg, S. (1980). *Clinical Studies in Infant Mental Health: The First Year of Life.* New York: Basic Books.

Freud, S. (1905). Three essays on the theory of sexuality. *Standard Edition* 7:123–243.

Ginsburg, B. E. (1982). Genetic factors in aggressive behavior. *Psychoanalytic Inquiry* 2:53–75.

Goldstein, J., Freud, A., and Solnit, A. J. (1973). *Beyond The Best Interests of the Child.* New York: The Free Press.

Greenspan, S. I. (1981). *Psychopathology and Adaptation in Infancy and Early Childhood.* New York: International Universities Press.

_____ (1989). *The Development of the Ego.* Madison, CT: International Universities Press.

_____ (1992). *Infancy and Early Childhood.* Madison, CT: International Universities Press.

Greenspan, S. I., and Greenspan, N. T. (1985). *First Feelings.* New York: Viking.

Hamburg, D. A. (1992). *Today's Children.* New York: Times Books.

Harlow, H. F. (1960). Primary affectional patterns in primates. *American Journal of Orthopsychiatry* 30:676–684.

Harlow, H. F., and Harlow, M. K. (1962). Social deprivation in monkeys. *Scientific American* 207:136–146.

Hartmann, H. (1950). Comments on the psychoanalytic theory of the ego. In *Essays on Ego Psychology,* pp. 113–141. New York: International Universities Press, 1964.

Heath, H., Scattergood, S., and Meyer, S. (1983). *Learning About Parenting.* Philadelphia, PA: Education and Parenting (revised, 1988).

Kagan, J. (1984). *The Nature of the Child.* New York: Basic Books.

Kandel, E. R., Schwartz, J. H., and Jessel, T. M. (1991). *Principles of Neural Science.* 3rd edition. New York: Elsevier.

Mahler, M. S. (1965). On the significance of the normal separation-individuation phase. In *Drives, Affects, and Behavior,* vol. 2, ed. M. Schur, pp. 161–169. New York: International Universities Press.

Mahler, M. S., Pine, F., and Bergman, A. (1975). *The Psychological Birth of the Human Infant.* New York: Basic Books.

McDevitt, J. B. (1991). Contributions of separation-individuation theory to the understanding of psychopathology during the prelatency years. In *Beyond the Symbiotic*

Orbit: Advances in Separation-Individuation Theory, ed. S. Akhtar and H. Parens, pp. 153–169. Hillsdale, NJ: Analytic Press.

Parens, H. (1973). Aggression: a reconsideration. *Journal of the American Psychoanalytic Association* 21:34–60.

——— (1979a). *The Development of Aggression in Early Childhood.* New York: Jason Aronson.

——— (1979b). Developmental considerations of ambivalence. *Psychoanalytic Study of the Child* 34:385–420. Madison, CT: International Universities Press.

——— (1988). A psychoanalytic contribution toward rearing emotionally healthy children: education for parenting. In *New Concepts in Psychoanalytic Psychotherapy,* ed. J. M. Ross and W. A. Myers, pp. 120–138. Washington, DC: American Psychiatric Press.

——— (1989a). Toward a reformulation of the psychoanalytic theory of aggression. In *The Course of Life.* Vol. 2: *Early Childhood,* ed. S. I. Greenspan and G. H. Pollock, pp. 643–687. New York: International Universities Press.

——— (1989b). Toward an epigenesis of aggression in early childhood. In *The Course of Life.* Vol. 2: *Early Childhood,* ed. S. I. Greenspan and G. H. Pollock, pp. 689–721. New York: International Universities Press.

Parens, H., Bockoven, D., and Goldberg-Moore, L. (1993a). Follow-up study: effects of prevention/early intervention parent–child groups. A preliminary report. (Unpublished manuscript.)

Parens, H., Giacomo, L., and McLeer, S. V. (1982). Toward preventing the development of excessive hostility in children. Presented at the meetings of the American Psychoanalytic Association, December 18, New York, NY.

Parens, H., Pollock, L., and Prall, R. C. (1974). Film no. 3: *Prevention/Early Intervention Mother–Infant Groups.* Philadelphia, PA: Audio-Visual Media, MCP/EPPI.

Parens, H., Scattergood, E., Duff, A., and Singletary, W. M. (1993b). *Parenting Education for Emotional Growth: A Curriculum for Students in Grades K Through 12.* (Work in Progress).

Parens, H., Scattergood, E., Singletary, W., and Duff, A. (1987). *Aggression In Our Children: Coping With It Constructively.* New York: Jason Aronson.

Parens, H., Singletary, W., Barcan, D., et al. (1986b). Evaluation of parenting activity scale: development and reliability testing. (Unpublished manuscript).

Parens, H., Singletary, W., Skivone, L., and Jessar, G. (1989). Toward preventing the development of excessive hostility in children: evolving methodology. Presented at the Mahler Research Colloquium in San Francisco, California, May 4, 1989; at the University of Pennsylvania, February 15, 1990; and elsewhere.

Parens, H., Singletary, W., Skivone, L., et al. (1986a). Toward preventing the development of excessive hostility in children. Presented to Research in Progress, Winter Meetings of the American Psychoanalytic Association, New York, December 20.

Post, R. M. (1992). Transduction of psychosocial stress into the neurobiology of recurrent affective disorder. *American Journal of Psychiatry* 149:999–1010.

Provence, S., and Naylor, A. (1983). *Working With Disadvantaged Parents and Their Children.* New Haven, CT: Yale University Press.

Rourke, B. P., Bakker, D. J., Fisk, J. L., and Strang, J. D. (1983). *Child Neuropsychology.* New York: Guilford.

Sander, L. W. (1962). Issues in early mother–child interaction. *Journal of the American Academy of Child and Adolescent Psychiatry* 1:141–166.

_____ (1985). Toward a logic of organization in psychobiological development. In *Biologic Response Styles: Clinical Implications,* ed. H. Klar and L. Siever, pp. 20–35. Washington, DC: American Psychiatric Press.

Sander, L. W., Stechler, J., and Burns, P. (1979). Change in infant and caregiver variables over the first two months of life. In *Origins of the Infant's Social Responsiveness,* ed. E. Thomas, pp. 349–407. Hillsdale, NJ: Lawrence Erlbaum.

Schorr, L. B., with Schorr, D. (1988). *Within Our Reach.* New York; Anchor/Doubleday.

Solnit, A. J., Nordhaus, B. F., and Lord, R. (1992). *When Home is No Haven.* New Haven, CT: Yale University Press.

Spitz, R. (1965). *The First Year of Life.* New York: International Universities Press.

Sroufe, A. L. (1982). The organization of emotional development. *Psychoanalytic Inquiry* 1:575–599.

Suomi, S. J. (1982). Abnormal behavior and animal models of psychopathology. In *Primate Behavior,* ed. J. L. Fobes and J. E. King, pp. 171–215. New York: Academic.

_____ (1991). Early stress and adult emotional reactivity in rhesus monkeys. In *The Childhood Environment and Adult Disease. Ciba Foundation Symposium* 156:171–188.

2

IMPLICATIONS OF ATTACHMENT THEORY FOR PREVENTION AND INTERVENTION

Byron Egeland, Ph.D. and
Martha Erickson, Ph.D.

A major effort in the area of prevention of parenting dysfunctions and child maladaptation has been the recent development of home visitation programs for mothers and their infants. One of the earliest programs was developed by David Olds and involved nurses making home visits for the purpose of reducing medical problems and teaching child care skills to new mothers. Olds and a number of others who have followed have based their programs on a public health model. Other approaches have been based on a mental health model (Greenspan et al. 1987), parent education model (Dunst et al. 1989), and a social support model (Barnard et al. 1988). The results of evaluations of home visitor programs are mixed, particularly with regard to having a positive effect on parents and on the child's development. Perhaps one reason for the mixed results is that the focus of intervention has been on the child or parent with little emphasis on their relationship.

Over the past twenty-five years, since Mary Ainsworth developed the Strange Situation procedure, there has been a considerable amount of research in the area of attachment between primary caregiver and infant. Recently there has been considerable interest in the clinical implications of attachment theory (Belsky and Nezworski 1988). We were guided by attachment theory in developing and evaluating a preventive intervention program for high-risk mothers and their infants. One of the major goals of the STEEP Program (Steps Toward Effective Enjoyable Parenting), a comprehensive and intensive program of home visits and group intervention for new parents, is to improve the interaction and relationship between mother and her infant. In particular, an aim was to improve the quality of mother–infant attachment as assessed by the Ainsworth Strange Situation.

We are currently completing a five-year controlled study of the effectiveness of the program, examining the impact of the program on several aspects of parental behavior, attitudes, and life management skills. Before describing the STEEP Program and presenting the preliminary findings regarding the impact of the program on attachment, we will present a summary of contemporary attachment theory and research. This study has implications for—and raises questions about—the application of attachment theory and the complexity of attempting to alter something as basic as the parent–infant attachment.

ATTACHMENT THEORY

Contemporary attachment theory is based primarily on the work of John Bowlby (Bowlby 1969, 1973, 1980). He was trained as a psychoanalyst and his ideas are similar to primary object relations theory. Bowlby's attachment theory is ethological in that he viewed the infant and parent–infant relationship within an evolutionary context, emphasizing the biological bases of attachment.

Bowlby proposes that infants are predisposed to form an

attachment to the caregiver, that the infant has a repertoire of attachment behaviors (e.g., sucking, crying, smiling, grasping) that facilitate this relationship, and that this attachment relationship serves a biological function, primarily the protection of the infant from harm. In addition to the attachment behaviors, which Bowlby claims are instinctive, he holds that infants have behavioral systems whose set goal is to promote and maintain proximity to the primary caregiver. Deviation from the goal activates the attachment behaviors and promotes proximity seeking.

At approximately 8–12 weeks of age, the infant is able to discriminate mother from other figures. At this time the baby directs proximity-promoting behaviors toward the discriminated figure. Near the end of the first year the infant becomes more active in seeking proximity to the attachment figure through locomotion as well as other attachment behaviors. During this time the infant is also more active in exploring the environment. Bowlby's set goal of proximity has been expanded by Sroufe and others to include felt security. Sroufe and Waters (1977) view the set goals of attachment as the extent to which the infant uses the caregiver as a secure base from which to explore. It is the security in the caregiver's presence that promotes exploration and it is the distress at separation that promotes proximity seeking. For the attached infant, separation from the mother is the occasion for anxiety. With this exploration and the emergence of representational abilities, the nature of the attachment changes from a relationship characterized by physical proximity to one described as a *goal-corrected partnership,* in which the mother and child share internal states and goals (Bowlby 1973). This goal-corrected partnership is reflected by increased mutuality observed in the relationship between the attachment figure and infant at approximately one year.

From this perspective, attachment refers to an emotional bond that develops over the course of the first year of infancy between the infant and primary caregiver. Attachment to the mother arises out of the interaction between caregiver and infant. The main issue with which we are concerned is the quality of the attachment that develops during the first year of life. The healthy attachment relationship is characterized by a balance of attachment behavior including proximity seeking and contact when the infant feels threatened and exploration when the infant feels secure (when proximity to mother has been established).

ASSESSING THE QUALITY OF ATTACHMENT

To assess the quality of the attachment between caregiver and infant, Ainsworth and Wittig (1969) developed a laboratory procedure called the Strange Situation. The procedure consists of a standardized series of eight 3-minute episodes involving infant–mother separations and reunions. The procedure is videotaped in a laboratory room equipped with age-appropriate toys. The order of episodes is arranged so that the infant experiences a series of increasingly stressful situations ranging from entering the strange room to being left alone in the room with a stranger and finally to being left entirely alone. By observing the quality of exploration in each of the situations, as well as the infant's behavior upon reunion with the caregiver, the infant is classified as either securely or anxiously attached, depending on the patterning and organization of attachment behaviors.

Infants are classified as securely attached (Type B) if the presence of the mother facilitates exploration and play prior to separation and if the presence of mother reduces distress and helps the infant return to play after a separation. If securely attached infants are distressed by separation, upon reunion they immediately seek contact, which is effective in terminating distress. When not distressed by separation, securely attached infants initiate active greeting behavior and appear happy to see the mother.

Infants classified as anxious avoidant (Type A) minimize the display of attachment behavior and shift their attention away from the mother to exploration. They readily separate to explore and play initially in the Strange Situation, but they show little affective sharing in their play. Most importantly, these infants display active avoidance upon reunion with their mothers, as evidenced in such behaviors as turning away, looking away, or ignoring the mother. This organization of the attachment behavioral system may serve to maintain proximity to a parent who consistently rejects displays of attachment behavior.

Infants classified as anxious resistant (Type C) maximize the display of attachment behavior and persist in focusing on the attachment figure to the exclusion of exploration. They seek contact but have difficulty settling upon reunion with their mothers. This behavioral organization may serve to maintain proximity to an inconsistently responsive parent.

THE DISORGANIZED PATTERN OF ATTACHMENT

Infants in the A, B, C categories have developed a coherent strategy for dealing with the stress of separation and reunion. In contrast to these organized attachment patterns, a disorganized/disoriented pattern has been reported. Recently, a number of investigators, particularly those working with maltreated and high-risk infants, have observed patterns of attachment behavior that did not fit into the A, B, C classification scheme. Crittenden (1988) noted that a number of maltreated children in her sample were displaying high levels of avoidance of the mother in combination with high levels of resistance. Main and Solomon (1986, 1990) found a similar combination of avoidance and resistance along with proximity seeking in their maltreated children. Unlike the children classified as A, B, or C, these children lacked a coherent and organized strategy for dealing with the stress of separation from and reunion with the attachment figure.

In addition to contradictory attachment patterns, these infants displayed bizarre symptoms in the presence of the attachment figure (e.g., anomalous positions such as huddled, prone, or depressed posture; freezing and stilling behaviors; and fear regarding parent). Main and Solomon (1986) describe this lack of an organized strategy and these abnormal behavior patterns as a disorganized/disoriented pattern of attachment (Type D).

ORIGINS OF SECURE, ANXIOUS, AND DISORGANIZED ATTACHMENT PATTERNS

Each of the organized attachment patterns (Type A, B, and C), as well as the disorganized attachment (Type D), is theorized to reflect the history of the interaction the infant has experienced with the caregiver. Mothers of infants classified as Ds have been found to have suffered severe loss, abuse, or other extreme traumas as a child (Ainsworth and Eichberg 1991, Main and Hesse 1990). Main and Hesse (1990) hypothesize that the parent's history of trauma and fear leads to parental behaviors that are frightening to the infant. They assessed mothers of Ds and noted behaviors that could be very frightening to an infant, at the same time encouraging the infant to approach and be comforted. Since the mother's frightening behaviors do not stem from the ongoing interaction between parent and infant, but are hypothesized to be the result of memories from the mother's past, these behaviors will be experienced by the infant as unpredictable and unexplainable in origin. The unpredictably frightening behavior by the mother mixed with responsiveness to attachment behavior may lead to strong conflict in the infant in stressful situations. This infant is confronted with the unresolvable conflict that the attachment figure is both the source of fright and the source of safety and security. If the conflict is strong enough, a possible outcome is disorganization in the infant's attachment system. Consistent with Main and Hesse's (1990) theory are the findings that infants classified as Ds were maltreated (Carlson et al. 1989) or were cared for by psychotic or highly depressed parents (Radke-Yarrow et al. 1985).

The history of the interaction of the securely attached infant with the attachment figure is one of responsive caregiving. A caregiver who meets the infant's needs in a consistent and responsive fashion and who provides a secure base will likely have a securely attached infant (Ainsworth et al., 1978). An interaction pattern involving maternal sensitivity and responsiveness to the infant's cues, communications, and attachment behavior is essential for a secure attachment. Using Ainsworth's scales (and those developed by other investigators) of maternal sensitivity and cooperation, we and a number of other investigators have found that ratings obtained during the first year predict quality of attachment at 12 and 18 months (Egeland and Farber 1984).

Infants classified as anxious avoidant have parents who are less sensitive and more emotionally unavailable and unresponsive than parents of securely attached infants. Parents of anxious resistant infants respond in an inconsistent fashion. A major goal of the STEEP Program is to help parents to be sensitive to their infants' cues and behaviors and to respond to these behaviors in a timely, consistent, and appropriate fashion.

COGNITIVE REPRESENTATIONS OF ATTACHMENT HISTORY: INNER WORKING MODEL

Up to this point, we have discussed mother–infant attachment in terms of how the infant has organized attachment behavior in partnership with mother. The quality of attachment is based on the infant's history of interacting with mother. In addition to the development of an organized pattern of attachment behaviors, children form representational models of attachment figures, of themselves and of themselves in relation to others (Bowlby

1980). These mental representations—or, as Bowlby calls them, inner working models (IWM)—are a set of rules that organizes how individuals see themselves and others and how they feel, think, and react within relationships (Main et al. 1985). Through IWM, children's affect, cognition, and expectations about future interaction are organized and carried forward into subsequent relationships.

Children construct models that best fit the reality of their situation. Based on a history of a responsive and available caregiver, the securely attached child has an internalized model of self as a worthy and lovable person, one who is able to actively solicit needed care. The child has a view of others as caring and trustworthy. The avoidant child is likely to have a representation of self as unlovable and of others as rejecting, unavailable, and untrustworthy. The resistant child has a caregiver whose responsiveness is not necessarily related to the child's signals; thus this child has an IWM of others as being unpredictable. Based on findings from the Mother–Child Project, a longitudinal study of high-risk children, we observed a group of preschool children with different attachment histories and found their behavior with peers and teachers to be consistent with their attachment history. For example, securely attached children approached teachers and peers with confidence and enthusiasm, while avoidant children tended to be less involved, especially with teachers (Sroufe 1983).

Although they are dynamic, as the term *working* implies, internal working models are thought to exist largely out of conscious awareness, possibly because much of their construction takes place before the onset of representational thought and language (Zeanah and Anders 1987). As well, with the development of representational thought and language, internal working models are thought to become an increasingly complex, extensive, and integral part of personality that guides perception, thinking, and behavior (Bowlby 1969, Zeanah and Zeanah 1989). This increased complexity and integration has been suggested as one reason that internal working models are more resistant to change in older children and adults than they are in infants (Zeanah and Anders 1987), as the individual moves farther away from the sensorimotor encodings of infancy that were the beginnings of the model. This is one reason for developing prevention programs for young infants and their parents.

Despite the basic stability of the inner working model, the existence of parents who were themselves abused but did not abuse their own children indicates that change may be possible (Egeland et al. 1988). Variables implicated in differentiating this group of parents from the parents who continued the abuse cycle were a supportive relationship with an adult other than the abusive parent in childhood or adolescence, a current stable and supportive primary relationship, or a history of successful therapy that had helped them work through and integrate the abusive experience into a nonabusive view of themselves. This work has provided empirical support for the clinical observations of Fraiberg and colleagues (1980) that maltreating mothers were able to stop re-creating their childhood experiences of abuse or neglect with their own children when they succeeded in integrating the emotions and memories of negative experiences into current understanding.

In our prior work with poor, high-risk, young mothers we have encountered many mothers who have been abused and improperly nurtured as children. Their expectations regarding their relationships with significant others were that they would be rejected, unloved, or abandoned. A major goal of STEEP is to help these mothers integrate the emotions and memories of negative childhood experiences and move toward more positive models of self and others. The notion of IWM has theoretical implications for understanding continuity of development, including parenting behaviors across generations, as well as potential implications for early preventive intervention with high-risk parents. A major goal of the STEEP program is to modify IWMs toward a more positive view of self and others.

Much recent interest in the IWM is due to the development of an interview for assessing IWM in adolescents and adults (Main et al. 1985). The Adult Attachment Interview (AAI) is designed to elicit memories of the individual's early attachment experience. The transcripts are classified into one of three major adult attachment categories, which reflect the individual's current state of mind with respect to the IWM of attachment. The attachment categories are: autonomous/secure, dismissing, or preoccupied. The degree of security implicit in adults' representational model of attachment is determined not on the basis of the actual events of their childhood, but rather upon the way memories and feelings about these experiences are organized. At the most general level, scoring reflects the degree to which an individual has access to feelings about early experiences, and insight into their effects. Typically, this is most clearly reflected in the degree of overall coherence in the narrative. Coherence is defined as fluency of ideation and speech, the absence of contradictions within the narrative, and—perhaps most important—the ability to match semantic generalizations of the relationship (e.g., my mother was loving) with episodic memories that in fact support such generalizations (e.g., a memory of mother responding to the child in ways that do in fact seem genuinely loving).

Individuals rated as dismissing characterize attachment relationships as being of little concern, value, or influence, and often have great difficulty remembering early experiences or describing them with any feeling or insight. They also tend to idealize their parents and, in doing so, obscure the reality of rejection and their own subsequent disappointment and hurt. Negative memories and their associated effects are excluded from consciousness. Thus, semantic generalizations are frequently at odds with the apparent reality of the relationship, and episodic memories are not available to serve as evidence for these semantic generalizations.

Preoccupied individuals still seem enmeshed in dependencies of their parents and still struggle actively to please them.

Incoherence in describing early experiences is high in this group. Typically, these individuals are flooded with episodic memories of early experience and their associated negative affects, but lack the structure to integrate these memories and affects and/or to place them in any perspective.[1]

THE STEEP PROGRAM

STEEP is a comprehensive and intensive preventive intervention program that has as one of its major goals the development of a good quality relationship between mother and baby. To facilitate a mother's sensitive and responsive care of her infant, we used a variety of educational, therapeutic, and support strategies. In general, we attempted to modify mother's inner working model, developed in her own childhood. Borrowing from what Selma Fraiberg has called "therapy in the kitchen" (Fraiberg et al. 1980), we attempted to help the mother face her own developmental history, examine how it affects her parenting, express the pain associated with her past and present circumstances, look at current choices and actions, and consider how she can now look forward to a more empowered way of living.

Design

Altogether, 154 high-risk mothers who were pregnant with their first child were recruited from the OB Clinic of Hennepin County Medical Center. The mothers were at risk because of poverty and associated risk factors such as lack of education, youth (range 17 to 25 years), single status, social isolation, and unstable life circumstances.

---

1. The AAI was administered to all mothers in the STEEP study at the time of the twenty-four-month assessment. At the current time, we have only coded thirty-five interviews, which is not a large enough sample to evaluate treatment effects on IWMs.

From the total sample of 154, seventy-four were randomly assigned to the STEEP Program and eighty were assigned to the comparison group. After enrollment, an extensive battery of tests including the Minnesota Multiphasic Personality Inventory (MMPI) and an interview were given. At 13 months, one month after the completion of the STEEP Program, mother and infant were assessed using interviews, tests, and videotaped observation of mother and infant, which included the Strange Situation. A similar assessment battery was administered at 19 and 24 months as well. The Strange Situation was given again at 19 months and a tool-using, problem-solving situation was given at 24 months. Only data from the assessment of attachment are reported in this presentation.

PROGRAM FACILITATORS: THE CRITICAL VARIABLE

The success of any prevention or intervention program depends to a large extent on the quality of the intervenor. Our facilitators were mothers who had some experience in working with low-income families. We attempted to hire individuals who appeared to genuinely care and who would be accepting of individual differences in values, beliefs, and styles. We also selected facilitators who had the ability to see the complexity of issues. In selecting facilitators, we asked applicants to respond to a series of case vignettes describing how they might approach each situation. These vignettes were useful in screening out applicants who oversimplified issues as well as those who tended to respond in an over-directive way.

PROGRAM FORMAT

The program includes home visits, beginning during the second trimester of pregnancy and continuing until the baby is a year old, and group meetings of eight mothers beginning just before the babies are born. A majority of the participants in STEEP have had many experiences of failure throughout their lives—in school, at work, and elsewhere. Because of their past failures, they are quick to feel failure now, particularly in a situation in which they may perceive someone to be judging the way they live. Because of their negative inner working models, the mothers often interpret their experiences in a negative way. Thus, from the first contact with a prospective participant, the STEEP Program is carefully structured to avoid sending a message of failure and rejection. For example, the enrollment process is designed so that the young woman is recruited during pregnancy, before she could have been judged in any way as a failure as a parent. The service is offered to her in positive, proactive ways as a source of support and education as she embarks on the new adventure of parenting. The person who recruits the participant is the one who will work with her throughout the program. We have observed that most women, when approached during the fifth or sixth month of pregnancy, perceive a need for some additional support during this time of transition, and recognize the offer of such a service as an opportunity to address their own needs and to try to give their child a good start in life. They do not seem to see the offer as a judgment that they have done something wrong (Egeland and Erickson 1990).

Prenatal visits focus on the mother's feelings about pregnancy and preparation for parenting. Our previous research indicated that mothers most at risk are those who feel totally positive or totally negative about becoming a parent, rather than experiencing a more realistic ambivalence (Brunnquell et al. 1981). This is a critical time for the "family life facilitator" to build a relationship with the participant. Because of their past history, many mothers expect to be rejected or abandoned by the facilitator. A strong effort is made to gain the mother's trust and hopefully begin to change her expectations about relationships. Facilitators do not give up on a participant even if she misses appointments. If a mother says she wants to participate, we continue to show up for as many visits as we have promised. Several mothers have commented that STEEP was their first experience with someone who did not give up on them. Our persistence and effort to prove we are available has paid off in many cases.

Whenever possible, the facilitator visited mother in the hospital at the time of delivery. Goals of the hospital visits were to demonstrate to mother that we were available and supportive, to encourage mother's interest in her baby, and to support her efforts to assume her new role as mother.

After several weeks of relationship building through home visits, the young mother was invited to join a group of seven to nine mothers with due dates close to her own. The group was led by the same facilitator who made the home visits. The group's sessions met every other week for three hours. Transportation was provided and the van driver, herself a young mother, also assisted during the group sessions. The sessions were held in space we rented in an inner-city church, which included a nursery and kitchen facilities where a meal and snacks were provided during the group session.

Each group sessions consisted of mom-centered and baby-centered activities. During baby-centered activities, the facilitator provided basic information about child development and parenting and guided the mothers in activities aimed at promoting a deeper understanding of the baby's behavior and developmental issues. (Specific activities will be discussed in the next section of this chapter.) The baby-centered time was followed by mom talk time aimed at encouraging the mothers to build supportive relationships with each other and empowering them to deal effectively with other aspects of their lives including stresses, relationships, school or work, and the use of existing community resources. Much of the discussion involved the mother's feelings and concerns about parenting, her baby, and her relationship with her baby. In keeping with attachment theory and research, we seized every opportunity to tie the mother's current feelings and experiences with her baby to her own experiences in childhood.

As we discussed in more detail elsewhere (Egeland and Erickson 1990), we found group activities to be especially powerful in bringing about a realistic examination of the past. For example, in one exercise we placed written messages on a table—messages that a child might hear from a parent, either through overt statements or implicit in the parent's actions. We then asked the parents to choose the messages they remembered hearing as children (e.g., "You're so cute" "If you do that again, I will hit you"). Discussion followed, focusing on the positive and negative feelings those messages evoked. Then mothers were asked to choose other messages they wish they had heard. Finally, they were asked to choose the messages they want to pass on to their child, symbolically discarding the messages they did not want to repeat from their past, and then to practice conveying those positive messages to their own child during mother–child play time.

Inevitably, there was at least one mother in the group who readily acknowledged the pain of an abusive past, and that almost always opened the door for others to begin to face and share their own stories. Some women, remembering an incident or feeling for the first time, were amazed at how they had blocked it from memory for so many years. Within this context we talked explicitly about the defenses—especially avoidance, detachment, and denial—that we all use to protect ourselves from pain, acknowledging the value of such defenses in enabling us to survive some terrible experiences. By discussing painful childhood experiences and strategies for coping with these experiences, we helped parents to recognize that the past does have a powerful influence on present relationships. This is different from psychoanalysis, where the patient seeks insight into past experience *knowing* that these experiences influence current feelings, needs, and behaviors. For our high-risk mothers, the first step was to see that their past has an influence on their present parenting behavior and relationship with their child.

Home visits occurred every other week between group sessions unless mother was experiencing some crisis, in which case the home visits occurred more frequently. Home visits provided the facilitator an opportunity to reinforce what was worked on in group as well as to individualize the program to suit each mother's unique needs and life circumstances. While the format of the home visit was necessarily flexible, the intent was psychologically therapeutic with an emphasis on exploring with the mother how her own developmental history and current life events influence the way she interacts with her child. Many of these discussions, especially in the early months, dealt with stress and crises in the mothers' lives, including problems with boyfriends, need for housing, and conflicts with her own parents or friends. These crises sometimes provided an opportunity to help mother learn to problem solve, but many mothers were unable to sit back and explore how these crises might be influencing their relationship with their child. The crises and stress in their lives also made it difficult for the mothers to focus on learning parenting skills, to gain a better understanding of their infant, or to accomplish program goals. Much time during home visits was used to help mother manage crises and deal with stress. It was necessary to reduce the stress before mom could focus on the specific goals of the program.

Following is a list of the major goals of the STEEP Program. These reflect the comprehensive and integrative approach we take with the high-risk families we serve.

1. To promote healthy, realistic attitudes toward pregnancy, childbirth, and child rearing.

   There are many aspects to this goal, including helping the mother understand that ambivalence is a normal part of the parenting experience and that relationships do not occur in a vacuum but are influenced in complex ways by present and past life circumstances.

2. To help parent understand child's development and form realistic expectations based on that knowledge and understanding.

   A goal is to help mother understand that behaviors have developmental meaning (e.g., sucking, mouthing objects, separation protest, experimenting with cause and effect, attachment to special objects, exploring own body, clinging, negativism and noncompliance).

3. To help parents respond sensitively to infant's cues and signals.

   The aim is to assist mother in recognizing the signalling capabilities of infant (e.g., crying, smiling, posturing, gaze aversion, shutting down) and to understand the importance of responding to baby's signals.

4. To help parent develop perspective-taking, particularly in regard to baby.

   Included in this goal is helping mother better understand how baby feels (feelings underlie signals and are often related to developmental issues such as those mentioned above) and call attention to how baby's behavior influences how parents feels.

5. To help parents create a home environment that is conducive to the child's healthy, competent development.

   The goal is to help mothers understand that babies need freedom to explore (baby proof rather than confine) and that stimulation, a predictable environment (and routine), and cooperative interactions (as opposed to intrusive style) are important.

6. To help parent strengthen support networks that can facilitate effective parenting and help parent build self-confidence.

   Our goal is to help mother effectively use the facilitator as a source of support (keeping appointments, expressing needs, initiating contact when needed, actively engaging in problem solving with facilitator).

7. To help parent develop life management skills that can minimize stressful events and help parent build a solid life for self and family.

   Much work here involves keeping appointments (use of personal calendar), money management (budgeting; low-cost options such as co-op grocery stores, resale clothing, public library, etc.), and planning ahead (preparations for baby's changing needs).

8. To help parent see options and feel powerful enough to pursue them.

   This goal involves empowering mother to be an effective parent, build a satisfying relationship, and live a productive life.

We have developed a number of activities to help mother achieve these goals. We cannot describe all of these activities in the space available; however, we will describe the therapeutic use of videotaping, since it is a major and somewhat unique part of our intervention. During group home visits, we often videotaped mother and infant in a variety of naturalistic interaction situations (e.g., feeding, playing, bathing). We then watched the tapes with the mother, using a careful, nonjudgmental approach designed to enhance mother's understanding of baby and their relationship, promote perspective taking, and increase her sensitivity to the infant's cues. For example, the facilitator would ask questions such as "What do you think your baby was feeling then?" or "What is your baby telling you?" The tapes provide an excellent means for helping mother to recognize and affirm her own knowledge of her baby. This strategy also affirms the individuality of each baby, focusing on what *this* baby does, rather than what a typical 3-month-old does. Videotapes also provide a good forum for helping the parent recognize and understand the reciprocity and mutual influence within the parent–child relationship. This strategy allows the facilitator and parent to be collaborators in discovering what a particular baby likes and wants and how those needs are expressed by baby.

IMPACT OF THE PROGRAM: RESULTS AND CONCLUSIONS

Preliminary findings suggest that the intervention had a positive impact on several variables associated with good parent–infant relationships. For example, the treatment group was found to have a better understanding of infants and their relationship with their infants compared to the control group. Mothers in the treatment group had lower depression and anxiety scores and were more competent in managing their daily life. They had higher scores on the HOME, which indicates that they provided a more stimulating and organized home environment. Unfortunately, the overall findings regarding the effects of the program on quality of mother–infant attachment as measured in the Strange Situation at 13 and 19 months were disappointing. The data analyses involved comparing treatment versus control groups, and then breaking the treatment groups down into two level-of-participation (LOP) subgroups and comparing these two groups to the control group. Two level-of-participation groups were formed by assigning all mothers who participated in fewer than thirty sessions to the low LOP (N = 38) and those who participated in more than thirty sessions were in the high LOP group (N = 35).

The number of STEEP mother–infant dyads in each attachment group is presented in Table 2–1. At 13 months the percentage of securely attached infants did differ between treatment and controls; unfortunately, the differences are in the wrong direction: 67 percent of the controls were securely attached and only 46 percent of the STEEP mother–infant pairs were classified as secure ($z = 2.42$, $p = .008$). Breaking the intervention group down into high and low level of participation did not result in a significant difference. Our explanation for this discouraging finding is that the intervention temporarily disrupted the attachment system resulting in an anxious attachment.

Looking only at the children classified as D (score greater than 5) at 13 months, we found significant differences ($z = -2.77$, $p = .003$). Unfortunately, the differences were not in the hypothesized direction. Nineteen percent of the control children were classified as D compared to 41 percent of the intervention children. These results are consistent with the overall finding of fewer securely attached infants in the intervention group. We would expect more Ds in the intervention group, if it is true that intervention temporarily disrupted the attachment system. Our hypothesis is that the mothers in the treatment group were more

Table 2–1. Attachment Classification for Treatment and Controls for Total Sample

	Control		Intervention	
	N	%	*N*	%
13 Month Attachment				
Anxious Avoidant (A)	6	8%	6	10%
Secure (B)	48	67%	29	46%
Anxious Resistant (C)	4	6%	2	3%
Disorganized (D)	14	19%	26	41%
19 Month Attachment				
Anxious Avoidant (A)	10	15%	5	8.5%
Secure (B)	32	48%	28	47%
Anxious Resistant (C)	4	6%	3	5%
Disorganized (D)	20	30%	23	39%

sensitive and responsive but these behaviors were not consistent enough to have an impact on the child's behavior. The treatment mothers appeared to be doing the right thing but at the time of the assessments, especially at 13 months, their relationship was in transition. One bit of evidence to support this idea comes from the significant correlations between 13 and 19 month D scores for the control group and a nonsignificant correlation between 13 and 19 month D scores for the treatment group. The significant correlation for the control group suggests that the D behavior is consistent with the child's history of interaction with mother during the first year of life. The lack of stability across the 13 to 19 month period suggests that there may have been changes in mother's caregiving and the interaction between mother and infant during the first year and these changes resulted in a transition in overall attachment patterns as well as disorganized behavior. Hopefully, the results of the observation of mother and toddler at age 2 will show a significant difference in favor of the treatment group.

At 19 months there was no significant difference between treatment and controls in terms of the percentage of infants classified as securely attached. The hoped-for delayed effect of treatment did not occur or was not yet apparent in regard to quality of attachment (see Table 2–1). There was, however, a decline from 13 to 19 months in the proportion of securely attached children in the control group ($z = 2.165$, $p = .01$) and a slight increase across this period in the proportion of securely attached in the treatment group. Looking at the number of children classified as D at 19 months did not yield a significant difference between treatment and control. The control group showed an increase between 13 and 19 months in the number of children classified as D and we were encouraged by the slight decrease in Ds across this period in the treatment group.

One possible reason that we did not obtain the desired effect on attachment is that our STEEP mothers did not benefit from our insight-oriented approach to intervention. Many mothers in our sample had severe behavioral, intellectual, and adjustment problems. In the total sample, seven mothers were found to have an IQ of less than 70, and six of these mothers were in the treatment group. Anecdotal evidence suggests that most low IQ mothers did not benefit from the intervention as much as higher IQ mothers. Those mothers seemed to require more directive teaching of specific and concrete parenting skills and probably needed more frequent, intensive intervention than we could provide. The results from the MMPI (Minnesota Multiphasic Personality Inventory), administered as part of the pretest battery, indicated that "the mean profiles on the validity, clinical and content scales, portray an overall picture of considerable personalilty dysfunction in this group of women" (Egeland et al. 1989, p. 261). Compared to the normative sample, as well as a subsample of adults with low levels of education and a subsample of pregnant women, the STEEP mothers had significantly higher scores on a number of scales. It was concluded that

> As a group, women in the STEEP sample appear to possess deviant social beliefs and attitudes. They display a reduced capacity for insight into their own behavior and the behavior of others and may feel somewhat overwhelmed and unable to cope with the problems they encounter in their daily lives. They appear to be alienated from society, possessing many misanthropic beliefs, expecting hidden negative motives behind the acts of others. They report a variety of unusual sensory experiences which, at least in part, may be attributed to the abuse of drugs and alcohol, known to be prevalent in this group of women. Their profiles suggest a history of antisocial behavior during childhood and adolescence, and a significant number may meet diagnostic criteria for an antisocial personality disorder as adults. These women also tend to have difficulty in controlling their anger and may become easily irritable and annoyed. There also are indications that they display considerable hostility in their interpersonal relationships. In addition, women in the STEEP sample report some depressive symptoms, excessive ru-

mination leading to difficulties in decision making, and a relatively large number of health concerns. [Egeland et al., p. 262]

In order to test the hypothesis that mothers displaying severe pathology on the MMPI and low IQ did not benefit from the STEEP intervention, we eliminated all mothers from the control and treatment groups who had IQs of less than 70 and scores on the clinical scales of the MMPI of greater than 80. Using these criteria there were thirty fewer mothers included in the analyses at 13 months and twenty-six fewer at 19 months. The results from using this reduced sample are presented in Table 2–2. As was true with the total sample, there was a difference between intervention and control in the percentage of securely attached at 13 months ($z = 2.50$, $p = .006$) and the percentage of children classified as D ($z = -2.77$, $p = .003$). For the reduced sample, there were no differences between treatment and controls at 19 months in the percentage classified as secure or the percentage classified as disorganized.

There were some interesting changes between 13 and 19 months. Over this time there was a slight increase in the percent of securely attached children for the intervention group and

Table 2–2. Attachment Classification for Treatment and Controls for Reduced Sample

	Control		Intervention	
	N	%	*N*	%
13 Month Attachment				
Anxious Avoidant (A)	4	7%	4	9%
Secure (B)	40	68%	20	43%
Anxious Resistant (C)	3	5%	1	2%
Disorganized (D)	12	20%	21	46%
19 Month Attachment				
Anxious Avoidant (A)	6	11%	4	9%
Secure (B)	25	47%	22	50%
Anxious Resistant (C)	4	8%	3	7%
Disorganized (D)	18	34%	15	34%

there was a significant decrease for the control group ($z = 2.21$, $p = .014$). Similarly, for the control group there was an increase in the number of children classified as disorganized (non-significant, $z = -1.63$, $p = .061$) between 13 and 19 months and there was a decrease in the number of Ds for the intervention group (non-significant, $z = 1.28$, $p = .110$). For both the total and reduced sample, the trends were clearly in the right direction. Using a different sample of high-risk families, we and a number of other investigators have found a decline in the percentage of securely attached children over a six month period (Egeland and Farber 1984). It was encouraging to find that the STEEP intervention appears to have reversed this trend.

In summary, the impact of STEEP on mother–infant attachment appeared to be the same regardless of whether or not the disturbed mothers were included in the analyses. Eliminating the low IQ and psychologically disturbed mothers from the analyses did not affect the results. For the total and reduced samples, more infants were classified as securely attached in the control group. The trends between 13 and 19 months, however, were encouraging. For the intervention group, there was an increase in the percentage of securely attached infants and a decrease in the number of children classified as disorganized. While these changes did not reach statistical significance, the trends nonetheless were encouraging, especially in the context of the other variables that were influenced by intervention.

DISCUSSION AND SUMMARY

One of the major goals of the STEEP Program was to improve the quality of the mother–infant relationship, particularly the quality of attachment as measured by the Strange Situation. Unfortunately, we did not obtain the desired effect on attachment. This finding is consistent with Osofsky, Beckwith, Barnard, and others who have attempted to improve the quality of attachment between mother and infant through home visitation. There are a number of possible reasons why we did not obtain the desired effect. The STEEP Program was comprehensive and intensive with a number of different goals having to do with parenting, empowerment, knowledge of baby, and quality of relationship with baby as well as with significant others. As we noted earlier, we have found a number of positive outcomes in the knowledge, parenting, and empowerment areas for mothers in the STEEP Program. In the area of attachment, our goal was to increase maternal sensitivity and responsiveness to baby and to help mother understand how her childhood history affects the way she feels about her baby and her relationship with her baby. Perhaps our approach was inappropriate or insufficient to effect such change with this particular population.

Our sample consisted of a number of mothers who were young and immature. Many were struggling with the developmental issues of adolescence, especially identity, autonomy, and individuation. This struggle for autonomy was often seen in anger, frustration, and dependency expressed toward her own mother. In addition, many young mothers were struggling with their relationships with boyfriends. For many who had boyfriends, there was often much conflict and tension (including physical violence) in their relationships and for mothers who did not have a boyfriend, many were preoccupied with finding one. All of these issues were important topics for discussion in both group and home visits. We have some evidence that indicates that many mothers made significant progress toward resolving these issues and we are confident that those mothers will ultimately have a better relationship with their child. Unfortunately, this effect was not evident in the assessments of attachment obtained shortly after the intervention program and six months later. Even though the time spent on these developmental and relationship issues resulted in the mother displaying more positive developmental outcomes, it sometimes seemed to be at the expense of working more directly on those program goals related to parenting and quality of attachment.

As noted above, a number of our mothers were severely disturbed or had low IQs. It is possible that our focus on parenting, and our emphasis on understanding how past history may influence current feelings and behavior, may not be feasible with parents who display such severe pathology and antisocial tendencies. Several explanations are plausible. It is possible that our program may not be suited for the most disturbed mothers in the sample, that our facilitators were inadequately prepared to work with those mothers, and/or that the intervention was not long enough or intense enough to have the hoped-for impact on these mothers. Certainly there are no easy answers for how to address the complex problems of many of these troubled young women. Future efforts at intervention and prevention will need to deal with the fact that this deviant psychological profile may be typical of so-called high-risk parents.

Another factor that seemed to make it difficult for some parents to work on insight and understanding was the extreme stress and chaos they experienced. As noted earlier, the facilitators often devoted much time and effort toward empowering mothers to manage the stress in their lives and to make choices that might decrease stressful events. We found on the twenty-four-month assessment that the STEEP moms were significantly better at coping with stress, and that the stress in their lives at the time was less than in the control group. There are a number of studies demonstrating a relationship between stress and attachment as well as stress and later parent–child relationships. We are optimistic that the improved coping, empowerment, and reduced stress found in the STEEP moms will eventually result in improved relationships with their child.

Finally, it may be, as Bowlby stated, that IWMs are difficult to change, especially for mothers who were maltreated as children and who learned to cope by dismissing attachment-related experiences. Many of the mothers acted out their childhood experiences, rather than committing them to memory. They were unable to see how these experiences may be related to current feelings and behaviors. This is consistent with Freud's (1914) view as expressed in his paper, "Remembering, Repeating, and Working-Through."

REFERENCES

Ainsworth, M. D. S., Blehar, M. C., Waters, E., and Wall, S. (1978). *Patterns of Attachment: A Psychological Study of the Strange Situation.* Hillsdale, NJ: Lawrence Erlbaum.

Ainsworth, M. D. S., and Eichberg, C. G. (1991). Effects on infant–mother attachment of mother's unresolved loss of an attachment figure or other traumatic experience. In *Attachment Across the Life Cycle,* ed. P. Marris, J. Stevenson-Hinde, and C. Parkes, pp. 160–183. New York: Routledge.

Ainsworth, M. D. S., and Wittig, B. A. (1969). Attachment and the exploratory behavior of one-year-olds in a strange situation. In *Determinants of Infant Behavior,* vol. 4, ed. B. M. Foss, pp. 113–136. London: Methuen.

Barnard, K. E., Magyary, D., Sumner, G., et al. (1988). Prevention of parenting alternations for women of low social support. *Psychiatry* 51:248–253.

Belsky, J., and Nezworski, T. (1988). *Clinical Implications of Attachment.* Hillsdale, NJ: Lawrence Erlbaum.

Bowlby, J. (1969). *Attachment.* New York: Basic Books.

_____ (1973). *Attachment and Loss.* Vol. 2: *Separation.* New York: Basic Books.

_____ (1980). *Loss.* New York: Basic Books.

Brunnquell, D., Crichton, L., and Egeland, B. (1981). Maternal personality and attitude in disturbances of child-rearing. *American Journal of Orthopsychiatry* 51:680–691.

Carlson, V., Cicchetti, D., Barnett, D., and Braunwald, K. (1989). Disorganized/disoriented attachment relationships in maltreated infants. *Developmental Psychology* 25:525–531.

Crittenden, P. M. (1988). Distorted patterns of relationship in maltreating families: the role of internal representational models. *Journal of Reproductive and Infant Psychology* 6:183–199.

Dunst, C., Snyder, S., and Mankinen, M. (1989). Efficacy of early intervention. In *Handbook of Special Education Research and Practice,* vol. 3, ed. M. Wang, M. Reynolds, and H. Walberg, pp. 259–293. Oxford, England: Pergamon.

Egeland, B., and Erickson, M. F. (1990). Rising above the past: strategies for helping new mothers break the cycle of abuse and neglect. *Zero to Three* 11:29–35.

Egeland, B., Erickson, M. F., Butcher, J. N., and Ben-Porath, Y. S. (1989). MMPI-2: profiles of women at risk for child abuse. *Journal of Personality Assessment* 57:254-263.

Egeland, B., and Farber, E. (1984). Infant-mother attachment: factors related to its development and changes over time. *Child Development* 55:753–771.

Egeland, B., Jacobvitz, D., and Sroufe, L. A. (1988). Breaking the cycle of abuse. *Child Development* 59:1080–1088.

Fraiberg, S., Adelson, E., and Shapiro, V. (1980). Ghosts in the nursery: a psychoanalytic approach to the problems of impaired mother-infant relationships. In *Clinical Studies in Infant Mental Health: The First Year of Life,* ed. S. Fraiberg, pp. 164–196. New York: Basic Books.

Freud, S. (1958). Remembering, repeating and working-through. *Standard Edition* 12:145–156.

Greenspan, S. I., Weider, S., Lieberman, A., et al., eds. (1987). *Infants in Multi-Risk Families: Case Studies in Preventive Intervention.* New York: International Universities Press.

Main, M., and Hesse, E. (1990). Parents' unresolved traumatic experiences are related to infant disorganized attachment status: is frightened and/or frightening parental behavior the linking mechanism? In *Attachment in Preschool Years,* ed. M. Greenberg, D. Cicchetti, and M. Cummings, pp. 161–182. Chicago: University of Chicago Press.

Main, M., Kaplan, N., and Cassidy, J. (1985). Security in infancy, childhood and adulthood: a move to the level of representation. In *Growing Points of Attachment Theory and Research,* ed. I. Bretherton and E. Waters. *Monographs of the Society for Research in Child Development* 50:66–104. (1-2, Serial No. 209).

Main, M., and Solomon, J. (1986). Discovery of an insecure-disorganized/disoriented attachment pattern. In *Affective Development in Infancy,* ed. T. B. Brazelton and M. W. Yogman, pp. 95–124. Norwood, NJ: Ablex.

——— (1990). Procedures for identifying infants as disorganized/disoriented during the Ainsworth Strange Situation. In *Attachment in the Preschool Years,* ed. M. Greenberg, D. Cicchetti, and M. Cummings, pp. 121–160. Chicago: University of Chicago Press.

Radke-Yarrow, M., Cummings, E. M., Kuczynski, L., and Chapman, M. (1985). Patterns of attachment in two- and three-year-olds in normal families and families with parental depression. *Child Development* 56:884–893.

Sroufe, L. A. (1983). Infant-caregiving attachment and patterns of adaptation in preschool: the roots of maladaptation and competence. In *Minnesota Symposium in Child Psychology,* vol. 16, ed. M. Perlmutter, pp. 41–81. Hillsdale, NJ: Lawrence Erlbaum.

Sroufe, L. A., and Waters, E. (1977). Attachment as organizational construct. *Child Development* 48:1184–1199.

Zeanah, C. H., and Anders, T. F. (1987). Subjectivity in parent-infant relationships: a discussion of internal working models. *Infant Mental Health Journal* 8:237–250.

Zeanah, C. H., and Zeanah, P. D. (1989). Intergenerational transmission of maltreatment: insights from attachment theory and research. *Psychiatry* 52:177–196.

3

DISCUSSION OF DRS. EGELAND AND ERICKSON'S CHAPTER

Patricia Nachman, Ph.D.

Dr. Egeland brings the perspective of a researcher and academic psychologist to his clinical intervention work with the STEEP Program. Working with large samples, he has been able to organize his data systematically into statistically significant groupings and comparisons. His primary data have been generated by information gained after more than a decade of work with the Ainsworth Strange Situation paradigm.

Dr. Egeland's research and clinical work are significantly influenced by attachment theory. The very fact that that theory has brought forth a steady output of research for two decades is a direct consequence of the success of the attachment paradigm in demonstrating that lawful relations exist between security of infant–mother attachment and later development in the preschool and school age years. Its superb performance as a *research* instrument has suggested the application of the Strange Situation, or modified versions of it, to clinical situations.

The Strange Situation is designed to evaluate the child's quality of attachment in terms of the use of the mother as a secure base. It does not incorporate systematic appraisals of other equally important aspects of the child's functioning, such as constitutional make-up, range of affect, predominant affective tone, tolerance of frustration and anxiety, resilience under stress, mother–infant patterns of activity/passivity, and infant and parent developmental history. These and other factors are important considerations that need to be incorporated into a clinical picture. By definition, attachment theory is not designed to provide such information.

The term *attachment* has a specific meaning in the research literature. It is a strong, enduring affectional tie that an individual makes to a specific other (Ainsworth 1969). Implied in this definition are the innate, genetically programmed aspects of behavior that allow infants to engage, connect with, and discriminate their primary caregivers. What makes them attachments instead of friendships or social acquaintances is the emotional core of felt security and perceived protection from danger in the presence of the attachment figure (Bretherton 1985).

Mahler's work, in contrast, is a *clinically* derived conception of early development. Her focus was on the formation and the differentiation of psychic structure and in understanding the genetic factors in psychoanalytic theory. Central to her thesis is the idea of the infant's ability to use the mother, not only for protection and safety as emphasized by attachment theorists, but for structuralization of the infant's newly developing ego.

For Mahler, separation is a gradual developmental process. Her theory of separation-individuation is primarily concerned with describing a developmental intrapsychic process through which self and object representations become increasingly differentiated.

Attachment theorists are more concerned with the psychobiological aspects of separation than with separation as a developmental process. Their focus until recently has been on receptor processes that interact with environmental stimuli to activate and terminate the activity of behavioral systems, particularly those having to do with parental protection. The recent shift in interest toward the more subjective aspect of attachment is stimulating a new area of inquiry that may bring attachment theory and psychoanalysis into closer alignment.

John Bowlby's work is of major significance when comparing developmental psychoanalytic theory and attachment theory. His conception of attachment theory was based on the idea that psychoanalysis needed a more methodologically precise format. Influenced by ethology and evolutionary biology and the work of Lorenz, he recast basic psychoanalytic themes having to do with attachment, separation, and loss in the form of potentially testable hypotheses. He provided a link between psychoanalysis and developmental psychology that ultimately had more impact on the field of developmental psychology than it had on psychoanalysis.

The work of Mary Ainsworth, an American research assistant of Bowlby's marked the beginning of this critical shift in developmental psychology in America. Prior to her work there were no procedures using the rigorous methodology of academic psychology to study the mother–child relationship. It is important to point out that Dr. Egeland's work stems from this line of investigation.

Ainsworth's work has proved to be a great enabler of further research. The research studies stemming from it have been steadily progressing in a direction that was inconceivable two decades ago. Currently, academic psychologists are attempting to think more complexly about how relationship patterns are carried and transmitted from parent to child (Main et al. 1985).

It is here that the idea of inner working models of a mother's (or father's) own early attachment relationship is used to document a correspondence to the quality of their infant's attachment to them. This work offers a framework for understanding associations between parental history and present parent–child relationships (Bowlby 1980, Bretherton 1985).

The idea behind inner working models of self and other is that they are developed in infancy and childhood and are generalized representations of the events experienced with the caregiving figures. These conceptualizations or models become incorporated into the personality structure of the child and serve as templates or guides for interactions (Bretherton 1985, Sroufe and Fleeson 1986). They are predicted to be relatively stable over time and to exert influence in adult life, particularly with respect to parenting behavior. To place Dr. Egeland's work in proper perspective, it is necessary to see how central Bowlby's theory of inner working models is to the clinical assumptions that guide the STEEP project.

The question of continuity and change in Bowlby's notion of working models is an important one. It provides a conceptual framework for understanding alteration of long-standing behavior patterns and it has important implications for therapeutic intervention. According to Bowlby, the inner models can be modified by new experiences that alter the underlying representational models of self and other. Change occurs through emotionally corrective experience in relationships. I might add that this idea has always been controversial in the psychoanalytic literature. Change can occur with repeated experience in a variety of relationships or through an especially strong emotional experience within a single relationship that disconfirms earlier acquired models.

With the idea of changing the inner working models of this sample of mothers, Dr. Egeland hypothesized that the mothers in the STEEP Program, who were afforded experiences designed to be corrective, would thereby overcome the effects of disturbed and disruptive aspects of their early lives. In consequence, their infants at age 1 year would be securely attached.

The concept of inner working models has its shortcomings when called upon to explain clinical phenomena of resistance, trauma, aggression, and ideas about psychic change. Problems arise when attachment theory is applied to the complexities of behavior that arise in a clinical setting.

Specifically, we can see how the idea of corrective experiences and the expectation of rapid change was central to the clinical assumptions and design of Dr. Egeland's project. It is significant that the program in which the mothers received many support services and experienced the availability of a sensitive adult ended 12 months after the birth of the infants. By all standards this is a remarkably short period of time to effect the expected changes. Furthermore, the end of the intervention aspect of the project may be assumed to have caused undue upset to many of the mothers.

Turning first to the main hypotheses of the study, results indicated that the control children did better than the children of STEEP mothers as far as the quality of the attachment to their mother was concerned. Moreover, the children who attended the STEEP Program the least often did better than those who attended more regularly. Dr. Egeland questioned this curious result.

While acknowledging an explanation offered by Dr. Egeland that by chance this may have been an unevenly distributed sample as far as IQ and mental health are concerned, there are several considerations about this result that deserve further comment.

The STEEP mothers and their children were evaluated right after their termination from the project. These were women from extremely disorganized backgrounds who, for several months prenatally and twelve months postnatally, had the attention of a facilitator who tried to build a relationship based on trust and availability, who put them in touch with childhood feelings, and who encouraged them to feel good about themselves at times when their aggressive impulses might ordinarily have gotten the upper hand, particularly with regard to their children. Also, they were made to feel that they were of interest and a part of a group because of their participation in the research project. I should imagine that intense feelings were aroused in the mothers when they experienced the project coming to an end, no matter how much in advance they were told that this was going to happen. Most likely the reverberations were different for each woman but without doubt some angry feelings were aroused. There is the possibility that the children at 13 months responded more like ambivalent and avoidant children (according to the Ainsworth classification) because of the increase in aggression their mothers were experiencing at the end of the evaluation period. This may be one way of explaining the high percentage of D (disorganized) children in the STEEP group at 13 months and then the decreased percentage of D children in this same group as they got older. If, for reasons of research design, the project had to end before the children were evaluated at 13 months, then, from the perspective of avoiding a possible source of contamination, it might have been better to provide a period of follow-up and adjustment to the termination before the evaluation began.

Dr. Egeland's view that the attachment process was disrupted in the STEEP women during the intervention phase of the project brings up the question of whether infantile longings and regressions were fostered in the mothers as a consequence of the Program's goal to rekindle childhood experiences and feelings. It was noted that the STEEP mothers appeared more immature and were less able to focus on their children's needs than the women in the control group. The possibility of an increase in regressive behavior in the STEEP mothers during the period of intervention may provide another explanation for the increase in D children in this group.

I am wondering why a continuous follow-up was not built into the project design at least until the children were in full-time school or until the mothers had achieved some improvement in their situation and their adjustment to parenting. If the basic premise of this project was to modify internal working models that developed maladaptively, to use Bowlby's term, because of excessive disappointments, loss, and feelings of helplessness, then sustaining the support services or some variation of these services, even on a limited basis, and not discontinuing them, seems more than justified and certainly responsive to the extraordinary needs of the women in the project. I suggest this while remaining aware of funding considerations and research priorities regarding the use of the

Strange Situation attachment categories in clinical situations. Perhaps future research will address the question of how inner working models change over time because it is exactly this kind of project for which the justification for ongoing services and long-term follow-up can be made.

Although the main hypotheses of this study about children's attachment classification were not confirmed, I hope that Dr. Egeland's disappointment in this finding did not extend to his view of the overall effectiveness of the STEEP Program.

The STEEP children did not change significantly in their attachment classification compared to the control group, but the mothers in the STEEP Program showed significant changes on measures of maternal sensitivity, on willingness to seek further therapeutic intervention, on building relationships with others, and in coping with stress. In addition, these same mothers in the treatment group had lower depression and anxiety scores and were more competent in managing their daily life than their counterparts in the control group. I cannot think of a more promising outcome and urge Dr. Egeland to give these variables a more privileged status and to use them more prominently as dependent variables or outcome measures.

According to Dr. Egeland's previous work, many of these variables were pivotal in making the difference between those mothers who could and those who could not break the cycle of abuse in the way they treated their own children. From this perspective I applaud the work done by the STEEP Program and feel assured that the mothers and children are benefiting even if the quality of their attachment cannot be measurably classified as having changed.

It is very difficult, if not impossible, to describe exactly what makes intervention programs effective. We can readily assume that most people—especially those who have had difficult beginnings—benefit from attention, concern, and the interest of others. Another essential and sustaining force in intervention programs is the curriculum and the way it is implemented.

We are observing the transposition of concepts that are basic to psychoanalytic theory into fields such as education and developmental research that have much more outreach and impact on the general population than does psychoanalysis as we know it in the consultation room. Important questions arise, therefore, about how principles from psychotherapy are understood and implemented in educational settings. This is an important area for psychoanalytic involvement and theoretical discussion.

In the "New Introductory Lectures" (1933) Freud spoke of the educational application of psychoanalysis and its importance for the future as ". . . perhaps the most important of all activities of analysis. What I am thinking of is the application of psychoanalysis to education, to the upbringing of the next generation" (p. 146).

Egeland's outstanding work as a research developmental psychologist and as the project director of a major clinical intervention program cannot but bring psychoanalysis and developmental psychology closer together. The work of the STEEP Program makes it seem even more possible for the two fields to grant each other's strengths and to learn from one another.

REFERENCES

Ainsworth, M. D. S. (1969). Object relations, dependency and attachment: a theoretical review of the infant–mother relationship. *Child Development* 40:969–1026.

Bowlby, J. (1980). *Attachment and Loss.* Vol. 3: *Loss: Sadness and Depression.* New York: Basic Books.

Bretherton, I. (1985). Attachment theory: retrospect and prospect. In *Growing Points of Attachment Theory and Research,* ed. I. Bretherton and E. Waters, pp. 3–35. *Monographs of the Society for Research in Child Development* 50 (1–2, Serial No. 209).

Freud, S. (1933). New introductory lectures in psychoanalysis. *Standard Edition* 22:3–184.

Main, M., Kaplan, N., and Cassidy, J. (1985). Security in infancy, childhood and adulthood: a move to the level of representation. In *Growing Points of Attachment Theory and Research,* ed. I. Bretherton and E. Waters, pp. 66–104. *Monographs of the Society for Research in Child Development* 50. (1-2, Serial No. 209).

Sroufe, A., and Fleeson, J. (1986). Attachment and the construction of relationships. In *Relationships and Development,* ed. W. Hartup and Z. Rubin, pp. 51–71. Hillsdale, NJ: Lawrence Erlbaum.

4

INFANT PSYCHIATRY WITH HIGH-INCOME AND LOW-INCOME MULTI-RISK FAMILIES, 1980–1990

Eleanor Galenson, M.D.

The paucity of therapeutic facilities to care for the vast number of emotionally disturbed and developmentally delayed very young children and their parents in this country is paralleled by an equally grave shortage of mental health professionals trained to carry out appropriate treatment programs. More training programs will have to be established, preferably under the aegis of mental health academic institutions, programs that will have to address a variety of issues including the nature of the basic curriculums to be taught. Is there agreement about curriculum, about the reliability of the various assessment and evaluation procedures now in use, and about a more basic issue—that is, the nature of the psychopathology encountered in various at-risk infant populations coming from the various cultural and socioeconomic sectors? Therapeutic facilities can provide effective treatment only if the treatment modality employed is an appropriate one for the type of disturbances to be treated.

It is the problem of defining some aspects of early psychopathology in the at-risk infant population that this chapter will address. Data derived from clinical experience treating middle- and upper-income infants and their parents in my private practice between 1980 and 1990 will be compared with data gathered in the course of a clinic-based therapeutic program for at-risk infants from a low-income population during the same period of years.

The groundwork required for defining early psychopathological states of infancy and early childhood was laid by the research and clinical experience of a pioneering group of psychoanalytically trained, extraordinarily gifted individuals. Anna Freud and Dorothy Burlingham (1973) described infants who were without families; Benjamin (1963) described various anxiety states of infancy; Kanner (1942–1943) discovered autistic disturbances; Spitz (1962) and Spitz and Wolf (1949) investigated the effects of excessive maternal deprivation, autoerotic-disturbances elaborated subsequently by Provence and Lipton (1962). Mahler (1958, 1963, 1966) and her co-workers (Mahler and Gosliner 1955, Mahler and La Perriere 1967, Mahler et al. 1975) studied and described the treatment of childhood autism and early psychotic states. Their contributions and psychotherapeutic approaches to emotional disturbances in older children were ineffective for treating these early disorders of the mother-child relationship. Therapeutic types of approaches were devised by a number of clinicians, particularly Mahler and her colleagues (1975) and Fraiberg (1980).

Other areas of infantile psychopathology (i.e., relating to infantile sexuality) were explored by Greenacre (1953, 1971), Roiphe (1968, 1973), Galenson (1971), Galenson and Roiphe (1976, 1980), Galenson and colleagues (1976), and Stoller (1968). The role of aggression in disorders of infancy, first addressed by Freud (1919) and later elaborated by Hartmann, Kris, and Loewenstein (1949), Loewenstein (1950), and Stone (1979), have been recently addressed by Bernstein (1983), Glenn (1984a,b), Galenson (1986, 1988), and others.

As the nature of the parental contribution to these disorders of infancy became more obvious, the role of the mother in the treatment of these disorders and the inclusion of the mother as an integral participant in the therapeutic work has gradually become recognized and accepted. Along with this development has come the realization of the profound influences of other environmental factors on the nature of early childhood psychopathology. While some of the clinical experience cited above was derived from treatment of children from middle- and upper-class families, other therapists were dealing with young children and parents from the lower socioeconomic sector. I believe the infant psychopathology encountered in these culturally and economically quite different groups varies considerably, variations that have not been acknowledged or systematically compared. Do the clinical features and developmental patterns in the different groups require modification of the therapeutic modalities to be applied?

An outstanding body of data derived from Mahler's separation-individuation studies of infants from middle- and upper-class families provided evidence for McDevitt's (1991) impressive proposition as to the very early emergence and long-term persistence of various types of conflict resolution. Meers (1970) studied infants and adults from a black ghetto community—a very different cultural and socioeconomic group. He reported a high incidence of ego deficits and widespread and serious sexual identity problems in the young children in this group—children who had not been identified as emotionally or psychologically deviant. In a subsequent report, Meers (1975) described and was puzzled by the frequency of traumatic sexual seductions of very young black children in the same population, seductions reported by both the children and their parents. Rather than being subjected to cover-up by the mother or psychological repression by the child, these sexual traumas were discussed rather freely with Meers; the mothers deplored the seductions and feared they would be repeated. The sexual acts were primarily carried out by relatives or visitors to the home, with whom the child was familiar, rather than by the parents themselves.

Meers also described a mutual exclusiveness of sex roles in the adult black population he studied, women and men going separate ways in their social and private, intimate lives. The adult sexuality Meers described rarely seemed to be a shared joy, but rather a source of drive release, coupled with a type of sexuality primarily sadomasochistic in character.

Finally, Meers discussed the widespread fear in the mothers of this infant population of any evidence of passivity and effeminacy in their male children, and a severe interdiction of anal erotism in children of both sexes. Masturbation was regarded as dangerous, symptomatic of mental illness, and therefore to be interdicted also.

Meers concluded that the various ego inhibitions, aggression turned back upon the self, and the prevalence of sadomasochistic sexuality were sequelae of the traumatic and precocious sexuality and seductions to which the infants and young children of the particular population he studied were chronically exposed. He concluded that the separation between male and female lives, both socially and sexually, is a deep-seated cultural characteristic that might result in the infantile psychopathology he described.

INFANT AND MATERNAL PSYCHOPATHOLOGY IN A COMPARABLE LOW SOCIOECONOMIC POPULATION

In the early 1980s, a unit was established within a hospital setting for evaluating and providing therapeutic services to emotionally and developmentally disturbed infants under 4 years of age. These infants and their parents came from the same low socioeconomic sector that Meers studied. Many of the findings reported below support Meers's reports. Early and constant exposure to sexuality that was closely associated with aggression, inhibition of anal eroticism in infants in favor of fixation to oral gratification, a high level of hostile aggression and a relative inhibition of early and late masturbation, extremely unfavorable environmental conditions of overcrowding, and other features that characterize the impoverished socioeconomic status of our population were constant aspects of the lives of this group, as they were of Meers's population.

Ego deficits, aggression turned against the self, fixation at a sadomasochistic level of sexuality, and failure to achieve true oedipal phase development were only occasionally absent in the young children with whom we worked over a 10-year period. Problems in establishing firm body boundaries and a stable sense of sexual identity were very common features in the infantile psychopathology our therapeutic efforts attempted to address.

During this same period between 1980 and 1990, emotionally disturbed infants and their parents who came from middle- and upper-class homes constituted at least one-third of my private practice patients. Just as there were vast differences in the environments and life experiences of these two populations of very young children, there were also consistent differences in the nature of the emotional and developmental disorders they presented, particularly in regard to (1) the stability of underlying personality structuralization, and (2) the nature of the balance between libidinal and aggressive impulses in their interpersonal relationships.

The treatment mode used in my private practice work with very young children and their families was derived from Mahler's (1955) tripartite model of treatment of autistic children—a model I then modified to suit the requirements of other types of psychopathology. Forty-five children, mostly below 3 years of age when first seen, were treated jointly with their parents between 1980 and 1990. Among the disorders the infants presented were disturbances in sleeping and eating, various types of developmental delays, problems in impulse control, incipient phobias, and various difficulties in establishing social relationships. Adopted children and twins were also seen.

While most of these very young children lived in intact family settings, some of their parents were contemplating marital separations or had already been divorced. All the fathers were employed, as were about two-thirds of the mothers. Many of the parents had been in either psychoanalytic or psychiatric therapy prior to the current treatment of the child. None of the parents had suffered psychotic decompensation, but at least one-third of the mothers and many of the fathers had been clinically depressed. None were drug addicted, but several parents suffered from alcoholic addiction.

During the same ten-year period, an infant therapeutic unit I supervised served the psychiatric needs of infants under 3 years whose families represented a severely underprivileged population. One-parent families, drug abuse, alcoholism, and violence were common—if not universal—aspects of their daily lives. The initial diagnoses of the children included nonorganic failure to thrive, physical and/or sexual abuse, pervasive developmental disorder, reactive attachment disorder, autism, various types of developmental delays, asthma, and other somatic problems. The diagnoses of the mothers included schizophrenia, chronic depression, mild retardation, fetal alcohol syndrome, intermittent psychotic disorganization, and drug abuse.

GROUP 1—PRIVATE PRACTICE GROUP

Among the children seen in private practice between 1980 and 1990 were a 23-month-old girl with language delay and anorexia, a 3-year-old boy with receptive but no expressive language, a 2½-year-old boy whose mother was severely ill and died by his third birthday, a 3-year-old twin boy with tantrums and serious aggressive behavior, a 3-year-old girl whose father had died during her third year of life, a 2-month-old adopted girl whose mother feared she might hurt her infant, an 8-month-old boy with a serious sleep disorder, a 19-month-old adopted girl whose mother felt no attachment to her, a 3-year-old girl who had been withholding her stool for several months, a 2½-year-old girl with severe separation anxiety and asthma, a 15-month-old girl with cerebral palsy, a 13-month-old girl with severe sleep problems, a 1¾-year-old girl with tantrums and stool withholding, a 3-year-old girl who refused to speak outside her home, an 18-month-old girl who had witnessed the rape of her babysitter, a 2½-year-old girl whose bouts of nonmanual masturbation had begun at 8 months, a 2½-year-old boy with incipient autistic withdrawal, and an 8-month-old infant whose parents were about to divorce.

For all these children (except the two who lost a parent through death) both parents were involved in the initial consultation and in much of the subsequent treatment of the child and family; however, the mother was usually the major participant in the ongoing treatment process. While the child was the designated patient, disturbances in the mother–child relationship as well as in the parental relationship quickly surfaced in our work with many of these families. Therapeutic intervention was aimed at establishing a more harmonious balance in the dyadic mother–child system and between the parents. One therapist worked with the child in the presence of one or the other parent while the second therapist (E. G.) saw the parents individually and assumed responsibility for the planning and direction treatment should take. Although support of the mother or father was often necessary during initial phases of treatment, the parental role was never usurped by either therapist. About one-fourth of the parents requested individual therapy for themselves, as they became aware of the extent of their own emotional problems in the course of conjoint treatment with their child. Although the parental relationships were often discordant and many of the parents were quite exhibitionistic, they did not consistently expose their infants to their own sexuality, nor was overt violence more than an extremely rare occurrence.

CASE 1—ANOREXIA AND ELECTIVE MUTISM

At 21 months, Maude had never uttered a word, although her receptive language appeared to be advanced. She had been cared for by a housekeeper from her early months while her mother and father were at work. She had been a poor eater from the start, and was still quite limited in her diet. Daily separation from her mother and father elicited no reaction from Maude, but she had severe tamper tantrums on other occasions, particularly when even mildly frustrated.

As participation in the three sessions each week brought mother and child together, Maude's severe separation anxiety and intense anger at her mother began to emerge. Maude's symptoms made life miserable for both mother and child and the mother's underlying depression soon surfaced. Maude's language gradually emerged as her mother began to recall her own early stressful childhood and her still unresolved ambivalent relationship to her own mother. Although Maude's mother and father divorced some three years after treatment ended, Maude continued to see her father. She had become an articulate, well-functioning child and, at 10 years of age, when her mother remarried, welcomed her new stepfather enthusiastically. However, she remained oversensitive to small slights from her peers and became moody and withdrawn at such times. Her mother pursued individual psychotherapy for some years, and was finally able to disengage herself to a surprising degree from her chronic ambivalent relationship to her own mother.

CASE 2—SEXUAL ABUSE OF A 2½-YEAR-OLD GIRL

Jenny, an ebullient, well-developing 2½-year-old, was brought for consultation because of increasing irritability and moodiness, disturbed sleep, social withdrawal, anger at her mother, increased thirst, repeated hand washing, and a sudden increase in doll play—symptoms that had first appeared six weeks prior to the consultation. This formerly self-sufficient little girl now demanded many bottles, refused to eat solids, and had obviously regressed in many areas of her psychological functioning.

A good deal of detective work by her parents brought to light the fact that her symptoms had begun to emerge following an evening spent with her 15-year-old male baby-sitter. They also learned that he had urinated in her presence and had attempted fellatio with her. The only way in which the father, a mental health professional, could deal with his own fury was to participate himself in Jenny's psychological treatment by initiating play therapeutic sessions with her, in addition to bringing her to see me at intervals. The sessions with her father were extraordinary examples of a very young child's capacity to play out and verbalize details of the traumatic event. For example, after playing a bouncing masturbatory game on her bed, she lay down, opened her mouth, pretended she was choking, told her father she was choking, and said, "It burns; get me water." Many subsequent references to biting and broken objects followed, and she then angrily accused her father of having broken her crayons. Soon she wanted to take off her underpants, complaining they were "hot." About two weeks later, she undressed all her dolls, remarked on their hair, shoes, and red hair bow, and asked for water to drink, explaining that her mouth was "hot." Her capacity to utilize such a variety of defenses—including displacement, denial, somatization, and temporary regression—as she struggled to master her anxiety over the sexual experience and to understand and replicate the sensations it had evoked was most impressive, particularly the progressive developmental step involved in her spontaneous, semisymbolic use of doll play. Six weeks after therapeutic intervention was initiated, Jenny gradually returned to her former good spirits; her appetite and sleep patterns were once again well regulated, and she began to speak of becoming a lady some day, like her mother. While there were reverberations of some symptoms when a sister was born a year later, her development seemed to be proceeding well after that.

While Jenny's capacity to deal with the traumatic event was most impressive, her father showed less resilience in coping with the damage he felt had been done to his beloved daughter. Although many of his own personal experiences had undoubtedly contributed to his unforgiving fury, this traumatic seduction remained the focus of the father's concern for his daughter for many years—affecting both his and Jenny's life in many ways.

CASE 3—ELECTIVE MUTISM IN A BOY, AGE 2-YEARS AND 10-MONTHS

Don had not yet begun toilet training, drank an almost unlimited number of bottles of milk daily, ate very few solids, carried his transitional object and several pacifiers everywhere, and communicated his needs and wishes through a rich gestural system and vocal intonations. He spoke no words. His hearing was intact and he seemed to comprehend spoken language. Severe separation anxiety, temper tantrums through which he ruled his parents, tooth grinding, and a strong preference for his father over his mother completed the initial clinical picture.

Don's mother, a chronically depressed woman, had suffered from a serious postpartum depression, leaving Don in the care of his father and housekeeper for the better part of his first 8 months. Following the housekeeper's departure, Don ruled over his father, who tended to grant Don's every wish. Don's mother had been considerably traumatized as a child by a prolonged illness for which she had been hospitalized and which had left her with a moderate deformity of one of her limbs. Adding to these early problems was her troubled relationship with her psychotic younger brother who had become decompensated some five years before Don's birth.

At least one of his parents participated in all Don's sessions during the first two years of his treatment. While his father was able to become engaged in the semisymbolic play that slowly emerged during therapy, his mother's continuing depression remained a serious obstacle to our attempts at modifying Don's fearful and angry relationship with her. We referred the mother for intensive individual therapy, a move that greatly facilitated our work with her and Don together. Gradually Don began to express his fury at his mother, his curiosity about her body in general, and about her distorted limb in particular. By his fourth year, expressive language was not only available to Don, but had become a powerful tool for controlling his family as well as his larger social environment.

Although we were quite certain that Don knew of his uncle's serious decompensation and deviant behavior, his parents could not agree to share this information with him. Symptoms of intense bodily disintegration and castration anxiety emerged again and again during Don's second and third years of treatment, followed by periods of regression to oral and anal satisfactions. By 6 years of age, Don still suffered bouts of anxiety in the face of changes in his environment; he explained that he preferred boys to girls and his father to his mother because girls and ladies had no penis and because his mother's distorted limb worried him. Despite his excellent school performance and close male friendships, a negative oedipal constellation appeared to be developing; Don was also burdened with the problem of knowing yet not knowing the family secret about his uncle. Although still somewhat symptomatic, Don's psychological development continued to advance during the four years of our posttreatment contact with this family.

SUMMARY OF PRIVATE PRACTICE CLASSES

While these three patients differed in their psychopathology, as did their parents, they lived within a family structure in which both parents were represented. The intactness of their family structure and the absence of chronic traumatic sexual and aggressive overstimulation probably played key roles—particularly during the latter part of the first year and during the second year of treatment—in determining the manner in which they negotiated their relationship with the mother. The presence of the father as a sexually active and emotionally involved partner to the mother apparently helps the child maintain a libidinal–aggressive impulse balance, which allows psychological development to proceed in more optimal directions.

GROUP 2—INFANTS FROM LOW INCOME MULTI-RISK FAMILIES, 1980 TO 1990

Mahler's (1955) tripartite treatment model for autistic children and her subsequent experience gained from her separation-individuation research, and Fraiberg's (1980) experience in treating young children and their mothers, confirmed the enormous advantage of including parents in therapeutic work along with their young children. The therapeutic unit was modeled on the Mahler and Fraiberg methods of parent participation. The data were derived from a population that suffered from intense social and economic deprivation; all the infants were at high risk. As both a therapeutic and research unit, several research questions had been proposed at the start, information that we hoped might contribute to certain aspects of psychoanalytic theory and to elaborating more effective strategies for early prevention and intervention with this at risk population of infants and parents. We hoped to identify the conditions of vulnerability and risk these infants faced, and the impact of these conditions on the nature of their libidinal attachment, on the development of aggression, and on aspects of ego and superego development. The children and their mothers attended three sessions a week. During each 2-hour session, individual therapists worked with each child–mother pair. A mother's group and home visits were other aspects of the nursery structure.

Between 1980 and 1990, 165 children and their parents were evaluated for psychological disorders; sixty-five child–mother pairs remained in treatment in our unit for one, two, or, in some cases, three years, and several more were followed in our other therapeutic unit for children between 3 and 5 years of age.

CASE 1—FAILURE-TO-THRIVE SYNDROME

The failure-to-thrive syndrome is a model condition to study the long-term impact of interrelationships among symptom formation, compromised family systems, inherent vulnerabilities, and early mother–child interactions. Failure to thrive is characterized by the absence, disruption, or distortion of normally occurring developmental sequences of attachment behaviors that serve to orient and anchor the infant to his caretakers and provide him with means by which to adapt to the wider social environment. Furthermore, although predisposing factors may be solely within the infant or the mother, many have pointed to the complex field of influences, including disruptive elements in the wider environment, which are usually involved. These wider environmental influences will be discussed in the following case.

> Ms. J., a depressed mother of four, was the only daughter of six children born to an alcoholic mother and a father who deserted the family periodically, and finally disappeared when Ms. J. was 12 years old. Her only other contact with him followed the murder of one of her brothers when Ms. J. was 18 years old. Communication with her mother was intermittent—at times almost daily but with other long periods of complete separation.
>
> Ms. J. could not express aggression directly, but would withdraw under stressful circumstances. Although her three elder children, all girls, had shown signs of neglect, the fourth child, a boy, was the only one who developed a full-fledged failure-to-thrive syndrome. Since Ms. J. and her three other children had already attended our unit, we were involved with Ms. J.'s pregnancy from the beginning, and with Larry J. from his birth. Although initially within normal developmental and nutritional limits, by 4 months Larry's physical growth fell below the 3rd percentile. He concurrently began to tune out the human voice, to avert eye contact, and to fall asleep moments after bottle feeding was initiated. Pediatric evaluation ruled out organic etiology, and it became evident that the mother was unable to

modulate her feelings of anger and emptiness as she fed and cared for her son. During his first few months Larry screamed and seemed enraged at times, but this gradually disappeared and his range of affect diminished as he seemed to be defending himself against his mother's overwhelming anger. Oral rage was replaced by oral inhibition—his food refusal. The rest of his development was distorted as well: He was somber, did not explore his world, and showed no interest in toys. By 8 months, Ms. J.'s interactions with Larry had become tauntingly ambivalent and erratic, with a distinctly sadomasochistic flavor, despite our intense therapeutic efforts with both mother and child. Larry's symbolic development was definitely delayed and his social relationships already distorted.

Within the next year, Ms. J. became seriously drug addicted and all four children were remanded to foster care, where Larry remained developmentally delayed and nutritionally borderline.

CASE 2—CHILD ABUSE

Fourteen-month-old Elaine and her mother, Ms. E., were referred to our unit because of verified physical abuse by the mother. During their first visit to our unit the child stood in the middle of the room staring fixedly at her mother, who sat morosely several yards away, cursing Elaine for being "crazy and stupid." When Elaine was placed in her mother's lap, the mother turned her upside down and squeezed her tightly between her knees and examined her diaper. Elaine remained emotionally impassive but obedient to her mother's commands.

Elaine had been hospitalized repeatedly for various illnesses and for injuries that were probably the result of abuse. Developmentally delayed in motor and symbolic development, she was closely bound to her mother in a mutually teasing and provocative interaction. After several months of intense therapeutic intervention with both mother and child in the unit setting, Elaine's development had advanced; she was no longer bound to her mother in terror and could accept help from other adults. However, serious developmental delay was evident in her continued oral regressive behavior, the absence of play and speech, and the mutual provocation that continued to characterize the mother–child relationship.

Ms. E. had been physically abused by her mother for many years; placed in a foster home during her adolescence, she promptly returned home and remained there ever since. Contacts with her father were very sporadic. When he occasionally visited the home, violent quarrels between the parents ensued and he quickly disappeared after each episode.

CASE 3—HOSTILE AGGRESSION IN A 2-⅓-YEAR-OLD BOY

Ben was referred to our nursery because of frequent tantrums and overtly dangerous aggressive acts toward his mother, other children, and animals. Ben had lived alone with his mother since his birth, his father having disappeared during the mother's pregnancy. Excessive crying during his first five months until he began to crawl had aggravated the mother, who could not tolerate disobedience and nonconformity. She herself was brought up by an angry, distant, and harshly disciplining mother.

Mother and child had become engaged in a battle of wills by the end of Ben's first year, and his anger in particular was vigorously squelched. Mrs. B. set limits that she could not enforce, causing fierce struggles between the two. Separations were extremely difficult for Ben, and his agitation would usually end in a tantrum. Yet despite these problems, Ben had an appealing quality that evoked positive responses in our staff.

After some months of attending our unit, Ben developed bedtime fears of ghosts. Games played in the unit about ghosts were threatening, yet obviously exciting. It was the relative quiescence following the ghost-play (his quest for a father) that indicated Ben's strong need for a male figure in his life. Indeed, he was able to form a strong attachment to a male therapist in our unit whom he referred to as his "father" within a few weeks.

Despite the initial severity of his illness, Ben's treatment was far more successful than had been our experience with most of these children, both male and female. The presence of a male figure appeared to have served both mother and child by providing protection to each from the unmodulated aggression with which they had both struggled.

SUMMARY OF UNIT CASES

In reviewing the cases treated in this unit, the results of treatment have been quite disappointing. We have been concerned by the prevalence of biting behavior—beginning at about 8 months and continuing into the second and third years—and other forms of aggressive behavior, both in the infants and their mothers. Overt affection between them was rare. Masturbation was also surprisingly uncommon in these children, except for several boys who would clutch their penis when upset or angry. Delay in semi-symbolic play and language development was ubiquitous.

Why have the infants in this group shown such intractable psychopathology so early? Is there a failure in psychological structuring during their earliest years and, if so, to what can this be ascribed?

DISCUSSION

In his evolutionary view of aggressive drive development, Stone (1979) argued that the prolonged nutritive dependence of the infant is dynamically related to the intense oral cannibalistic fantasies that begin at least with the onset of teething. Ordinarily, these fantasies are then deployed from the mouth and teeth to the hands, leaving the mouth free for the development of the uniquely human function of speech. Stone suggests that oral rage is then replaced by the frustrations related to sphincter control of the second year, with its characteristic mode of functioning. The specifically human practice of toilet training is, in Stone's view, an important source of narcissistic mortification, which adds a specific increment of object-directed anger.

Since the struggle for impulse control becomes an *integral* one with the onset of anal phase development, Stone believes anal phase development is particularly significant for psychic structuralization. Stone places great emphasis upon the normal passage through anal phase development as necessary for the elaboration of nonverbal fantasy and other types of thought—*before* they are transformed into play and language.

If one accepts Stone's view of aggressive drive development, it seems plausible that a disturbance of the aggressive-libidinal balance during the latter part of the first year and the entire second year, either because of earlier trauma (physical or psychological) or a disturbance in the mother–child relationship, specifically in regard to the areas of libidinal and aggressive anal impulses, would pose a serious threat to ongoing psychic structuralization affecting all spheres.

Freud (1920) described the early months of the second year as the stage of development when the destructive force of the aggressive drive increases, requiring the mobilization of a range of defensive maneuvers to preserve the infant's attachment to the mother. The defenses of displacement and turning aggression against the self, while maintaining the basic attachment to the object, do not modulate the force of the aggressive drive. Other defenses such as somatization, which undermines bodily integrity, and regression and splitting, which compromise ego integrity, are very frequently called into play during the same era.

The only defense that succeeds in modulating the destructive force of the aggressive drive itself is the eroticization of aggression, the defense that inevitably leads to the compromise formation known as sadomasochism, or protosadomashocism, as some prefer to designate it, if aggression has been intensified either by internal or external influences.

It seems plausible that at the beginning of the second year

family structure and other environmental factors surrounding the disadvantaged infant play a critical role in determining the developmental direction of the ambivalent relationship experienced by both mother and child. If the father is an active family participant, if the mother had experienced her own father as a source of libidinal attachment who provided a balance for her hostile aggression to her own mother, and if the environment does not constantly overstimulate sexuality and aggression, the mother can then deal with the toddler's ambivalence without retaliatory interchange. The child's attachment to the father normally serves to deflect and modify his or her aggression away from the mother during the second year. Girls then turn to the father, erotically preparing for the future oedipal attachment, while boys must disidentify with the mother, a process that tends to intensify hostile aggression in them. Looking to the father for a positive libidinal attachment, the boy also seeks to identify with his father's phallic attributes in order to disengage from his mother.

However, if the family structure does not include the father, and especially if the environment is both aggressively and sexually overstimulating, mother and child cannot solve their mutual, overtly hostile ambivalence through the normal channels. Erotization of aggression may then be called into play as a major defense against the threat to the maternal relationship. In this eventuality the sadomasochistic quality will extend to other relationships as well, interfering with the advance to an oedipal type of attachment. Genitality assumes pregenital characteristics, and masturbation would be expected to be inhibited and distorted.

Are there other effects of the fusion of the two instinctual drives? Here I believe Stone's views regarding the formation of psychic structure are extremely helpful. If the internal struggle between anal phase impulses is prematurely curtailed or distorted, it seems likely that psychic structuralization would be distorted as well. The children whose fathers are not available at the critical second year period and whose anal eroticism is discouraged as dangerously passive, do not traverse normal anal phase development. Their semisymbolic play, normally available in the repertoire of the 16- to 18-month-old child for the elaboration of fantasy, is absent, and they fail to develop language at the appropriate time. These developmental delays interfere, I believe, not only with the capacity to elaborate internal fantasy but with other types of thought processes as well. Impulse leads directly to action in them, rather than to the delay, which is essential for the structuralization required for the development of mentation.

Failure to sufficiently resolve hostile ambivalence to the mother seems to interfere with the young child's capacity to utilize masturbation in the service of binding aggression and establishing a secure sense of gender identity. Furthermore, parental inhibition of direct masturbatory discharge requires substitution of other behavior, which often proves self-destructive and curtails the capacity to achieve a truly oedipal level of sexual development.

CONCLUSION

Many factors must be considered in connection with prevention and treatment of emotional and development disturbances in disadvantaged young children and their parents. The vast economic and sociological problems certainly contribute in large part to the crippling personality disorders affecting this population of young children.

More trained mental health professionals are a prime requirement if we are to mount a successful program for treating this vast group of very young but already deviant children. The family structure within which they begin their lives, with its social and sexual separation of males from females, contributes to an environment that is overstimulating sexually and aggressively—features that interfere with the very young child's capacity to learn to modulate aggressive and sexual impulses. Regression to or fixation at oral types of gratification, along with the tendency to foster immediate impulse discharge in the form of action, interfere with ongoing psychic structuralization. Early fusion of aggressive and sexual impulses encourages the development of a sadomasochistic type of object relationship and sexual identity confusion, which interferes with the achievement of truly oedipal object relationships. The nature of this psychopathology requires special modification of the therapeutic approach if such programs are to be therapeutically effective.

A full-day therapeutic experience in which the young child spends the greater part of his early years within a structured program carried out under the supervision of trained mental health professionals would provide a model that I believe has not as yet been attempted. The mothers of these children should also be given the opportunity for collateral therapeutic treatment appropriate to their own needs. Until such a model has been put into practice and carefully evaluated by follow-up studies, we cannot know that it will be effective. I believe the time has come to face the unpleasant reality that none of our current therapeutic models has as yet proven sufficiently effective in the early intervention and treatment of the psychological disorders of the seriously at-risk infants from this economically and socially deprived segment of our population.

REFERENCES

Benjamin, J. D. (1963). Further comments on some developmental aspects of anxiety. In *Counterpoint: Libidinal Object and Subject*, ed. H. S. Gaskill, pp. 121–153. New York: International Universities Press.

Bernstein, I. (1983). Masochistic pathology and feminine development. *Journal of the American Psychoanalytic Association* 31:467–486.

Fraiberg, S. (1980). *Clinical Studies in Infant Mental Health.* New York: Basic Books.

Freud, A., and Burlingham, D. (1973). Infants without families. Reports on the Hampstead nurseries. *The Writings of Anna Freud*, vol. 3, pp. 543–564. New York: International Universities Press.

Freud, S. (1919). A child is being beaten. *Standard Edition* 17:177–204.

_____ (1920). Beyond the pleasure principle. *Standard Edition* 18:7–64.

Galenson, E. (1971). A consideration of the nature of thought in childhood play. In *Separation-Individuation, Essays in Honor of Margaret S. Mahler,* ed. J. B. McDevitt and C. F. Settlage, pp. 41–48. New York: International Universities Press.

_____ (1986). Some thoughts about infant psychopathology and aggressive development. *International Review of Psycho-Analysis* 13:349–354.

_____ (1988). The precursors of masochism: protomasochism. In *Masochism: Current Psychoanalytic Perspectives,* ed. R. A. Glick and D. I. Meyers, pp. 189–204. Hillsdale, NJ: Analytic Press.

Galenson, E., Miller, R., and Roiphe, H. (1976). The choice of symbols. *Journal of the Academy of Child Psychiatry* 15:83–96.

Galenson, E., and Roiphe, H. (1971). The impact of early sexual discovery on mood, defensive organization and symbolization. In *The Psychoanalytic Study of the Child* 26:195–216. New York: International Universities Press.

_____ (1976). Some suggested revisions concerning early female development. *Journal of the American Psychoanalytic Association* 24:29–57.

_____ (1980). The preoedipal development of the boy. *Journal of the American Psychoanalytic Association* 28:805–828.

Glenn, J. (1984a). A note on loss, pain, depression and masochism in children. *Journal of the American Psychoanalytic Association* 32:65–75.

_____ (1984b). Psychic trauma and masochism. *Journal of the American Psychoanalytic Association* 32:357–380.

Greenacre, P. (1953). Certain relationships between fetishism and the faulty development of the body image. In *Psychoanalytic Study of the Child* 8:79–98. New York: International Universities Press.

_____ (1971). Early physical determinants in the development of the sense of identity. In *Emotional Growth,* vol. 1, ed. P. Greenacre, pp. 113–127. New York: International Universities Press.

Hartmann, H., Kris, E., and Loewenstein, R. M. (1949). Notes on the theory of aggression. *Psychoanalytic Study of the Child* 3/4:9–36. New York: International Universities Press.

Kanner, L. (1942–43). Autistic disturbances of affective contact. *The Nervous Child* 2:217–250.

Loewenstein, R. (1950). Conflict over autonomous ego development during the phallic phase. *Psychoanalytic Study of the Child* 5:47–52. New York: International Universities Press.

Mahler, M. S. (1958). Autism and symbiosis: two extreme disturbances of identity. *International Journal of Psycho-Analysis* 39:77–83.

_____ (1963). Thoughts about development and individuation. In *Psychoanalytic Study of the Child* 18:307–324. New York: International Universities Press.

_____ (1966). Notes on the development of basic moods: the depressive affect. In *Psychoanalysis—A General Psychology: Essays in Honor of Heinz Hartmann,* ed. R. M. Loewenstein, L. M. Newman, M. Schur, and A. J. Solnit, pp. 152–168. New York: International Universities Press.

Mahler, M. S., and Gosliner, B. J. (1955). On symbiotic child psychosis: genetic, dynamic and restitutive aspects. *Psychoanalytic Study of the Child* 10:195–212. New York: International Universities Press.

Mahler, M. S., and LaPerriere, K. (1967). Development of "defense" from biological and symbiotic precursors: adaptive and maladaptive aspects. *Journal of the American Psychoanalytic Association* 15:130–149.

Mahler, M. S., Pine, F., and Berman, A. (1975). *The Psychological Birth of the Human Infant.* New York: Basic Books.

McDevitt, J. (1991). Contributions of separation-individuation through the understanding of psychopathology during the prelatency years. In *Beyond the Symbiotic Orbit: Advances in Separation-Individuation. Essays in Honor of Selma Kramer, M.S.*, ed. S. A. Akhtar and H. Parens, pp. 153–169. Hillsdale, NJ: Analytic Press.

Meers, D. R. (1970). Contributions of a ghetto culture to symptom formation: psychoanalytic studies of ego anomalies in childhood. *Psychoanalytic Study of the Child* 25:209–230. New York: International Universities Press.

_____ (1975). Precocious sexuality and masturbation: sexuality and the ghetto. In *Masturbation from Infancy to Senescence,* ed. I. M. Marcus and J. J. Francis, pp. 441–438. New York: International Universities Press.

Provence, S., and Lipton, R. (1962). *Infants in Institutions.* New York: International Universities Press.

Roiphe, H. (1968). On an early genital phase. *Psychoanalytic Study of the Child* 23:348–365. New York: International Universities Press.

_____ (1973). The infantile fetish. *Psychoanalytic Study of the Child* 28:147–166. Madison, CT: International Universities Press.

Spitz, R. A. (1962). Autoerotism re-examined. *Psychoanalytic Study of the Child* 17:283–315. New York: International Universities Press.

Spitz, R. A., and Wolf, K. M. (1949). Autoerotism: some empirical findings and hypotheses on three of its manifestations in the first year of life. *Psychoanalytic Study of the Child* 3/4:85–120. New York: International Universities Press.

Stoller, R. J. (1968). *Sex and Gender.* New York: Science House.

Stone, L. (1979). Remarks on certain unique conditions of human aggression (the hand, speech, and the use of fire). *Journal of the American Psychoanalytic Association* 27:27–33.

5

DISCUSSION OF DR. GALENSON'S CHAPTER

J. Alexis Burland, M.D.

Will there be prevention in mental health EVER? That question is testimony to a certain frustration felt by experts in child development. We have known, as a science, of the importance of childhood in the life cycle for about a century, and in the past fifty years there has been an explosion of research and new information on the topic. But we still struggle to find effective and operable means to apply this information where it might do the most good. Dr. Galenson addresses this struggle directly. In response to her chapter I will comment on three of the subjects with which she has dealt: first, what is meant by the term *prevention;* second, what is the influence of community-based child rearing practices; and third, some thoughts on Dr. Galenson's formulations concerning the role of the father in the epigenesis of destructive aggression in children.

PREVENTION, EARLY INTERVENTION, AND TREATMENT

According to the Oxford English Dictionary, *prevention* means: "to act before, in anticipation of, or in preparation for . . . a future event. . . ." Here, the future event is the psychological birth of the human infant, as Mahler phrased it (Mahler et al. 1975). What is distressing and puzzling is that that future event has already been prepared for, naturally, by inherent constitutional givens. As Dr. Egeland has reminded us: The human infant is born prewired to seek out and interact with a "good enough" mother, and is also born with considerable resilience so as to be able to adapt as needed (Egeland, Chapter 2, this volume). Further, mothers are prewired to be invested in and empathically attuned to their infants' developmental needs. We find, however, in the real world, that such constitutional preventative measures are all too often overridden by a variety of factors. In spite of the prewiring and the infant's resilience, things can go wrong, and the psychological birth process can get derailed.

A young man struggling in analysis to reverse the self-loathing caused by his mother's angry rejection of him has been slowly discovering some of his assets and strengths, realizing that he has many good qualities that managed to escape the destructive impact of his mother's rejection by "going into hiding." But his discovery of these previously sequestered inherent strengths puzzled him as much as it pleased him. In a philosophical tone, but with much affective distress, he said: "Why is it that I, as an infant, was so effectively prewired, but my mother, for her job as mother, was not?" He raised a fair question. Though we cannot tell him why it is so, it is nevertheless a sad fact: What nature has provided to facilitate the development of the newborn human infant is all too often distressingly vulnerable.

The title of this book uses the word *prevention;* in her

chapter, Dr. Galenson describes situations in which the natural preventative measures have been overcome, and the unnatural has already supplanted the ideal for these children. They are already symptomatic. Whether due to idiosyncratic or social factors, or both, her patients' parents lost their ability to behave according to their inherent biological potential. The phrase *early intervention* is often used, related to the age of the child. But in both her high-income and low-income groups, the children's problems were but a link in a multigenerational chain of many years' duration. I am not sure that the word prevention is in fact ever truly appropriate in matters of mental health. I am reminded of the experiences of Anna Freud, Melanie Klein, and their colleagues in Vienna in the '20s. Realizing the critical importance of the infantile neurosis as a causative factor in adult neurosis, they began working with children in the hopes of preventing adult neuroses. But instead, they found children already in need of treatment for themselves, and child analysis as a treatment modality was born.

For over a decade I was a consultant at a variety of mental health and social agencies in the impoverished inner city, including one that attempted to each young, teenage, single mothers child rearing practices. It was conceived of as a preventative program, so much so that the program's initial philosophy was that the young mothers and their babies were not to be seen as "patients." This was in spite of the fact that the mothers were referred to us by their physicians or schools as high risk. Nevertheless, within weeks the entire staff realized that almost all of the young mothers were appropriately thought of as patients. In fact, the more dysfunctional mothers in our high-risk group—with their failures in parenting skills and resistances to our efforts at improving them—converted our preventative program into a laboratory for the observational study of the developmental impact of maternal deprivation. Most of my data on the effects of maternal deprivation comes from my observations of the most dysfunctional mother–infant pairs in that group.

There is an interesting and telling philosophical side to this matter. Much of my time as a consultant to that program was spent trying to deal with staff morale, often at a low level in response to their more intransigent clients. Although some clients did well, a subset of them did not, and they depressed, angered, and puzzled the staff, drawing the greater amount of their attention and energies. These mothers seemed a contradiction to human nature. If the essence of a *good enough facilitating environment*—to combine two of Winnicott's terms—is an expression of constitutionally determined, inherent capabilities, how can it be that for some mothers we needed a preventative program to assure these capabilities? How can there exist in nature self-perpetuating multigenerational behaviors so destructive to the human spirit, which, I believe, is firmly rooted in the first months of life? It was as though we took for granted that nature knew what it was doing, despite the clinical data that was evident that nature sometimes seems to work against itself. These questions raised other questions, related more specifically to our observations of some of the more dysfunctional mother–infant pairs: why is it that the topic of child rearing has been so neglected? Why is it that the behavioral sciences only began to explore this subject over the last hundred years, even though humanlike animals have been rearing their infants for 1,300,000 years, Homo sapiens for 75,000 years? Novelists such as Dickens have been aware that child rearing practices could be less than ideal, as have social critics and theologians; why not behavioral scientists? When we think of the rush of excitement and joy we feel when we see a beaming infant, gurgling and chortling with glee, legs kicking the air in excitement, engaged in an enchanting game of kootchy-koo with a doting mother, or when we think of how a baby in distress can reduce the strongest of us to tears, how is it that the study of such utterly beguiling and captivating creatures as infants is so much younger than the study of rocks, or flowers, or birds? Not surprisingly, we found no answers to these rhetorical questions in our staff meetings. It seemed to us that we were observing people destroying themselves, and in ways that few of us could understand. But we dismissed as naive the notion that we were a preventative program.

THE ROLE OF CULTURE

Dr. Galenson divided her research subjects into two cohorts—high income and low income—and stressed the multirisk situation for infants born into low socioeconomic families. It should be kept in mind that low income and multirisk low income are broad categorizations. There are several kinds of low-income multirisk families, each requiring a somewhat different kind of program. It has long been known that growing up in a multirisk family is bad for children: Anna Freud began her work with children from multirisk families in Vienna, and continued with a similar population at Hampstead. August Aichhorn began his psychoanalytic work with delinquent adolescents from similar backgrounds.

It became painfully clear to me in my years of work in the low-income neighborhoods of Philadelphia that in many of the multirisk families there was a self-perpetuating, obstinate set of destructive beliefs about child-rearing practices (Burland 1984, 1986). This was a subculture of maternal deprivation, defining subculture as a system of community-based norms that included the promulgation of child-rearing practices that served to perpetuate the system. That system was in place in the community of high risk mothers with whom I worked. Since most young mothers in our parenthood training program could not get along with their own mothers, it was the maternal grandmother who taught them about child rearing. Among the lessons they taught were: never pick up crying babies; it spoils them, it lies to them about the real world by telling them that someone cares about their pain. In fact, when babies cry, it is best to really give them something to cry about—a beating. (Every year in Philadelphia we hear of several infants who are beaten to death for refusing to stop crying when told to do so.) Never pick up a crying baby boy or he will become homosexual. Young mothers compete to have their babies walking early, toilet trained early, and in day care as soon as possible; self-reliance is important, and dependency is bad. Expect two-year-olds to get themselves up, fed, dressed, and to the bus stop for Head Start programs. Children are mean by nature; "bad" things are done on purpose, and out of spite.

One young mother was unable to get her infant to stop crying; her case worker took the baby from her, and by gently rocking him and talking to him, got him to cease. The mother was furious, grabbed her baby back, and hit him, complaining that he had responded to the worker only to humiliate her, since he must hate her. The mothers are taught to expect and demand instant compliance and love from their children, even though they themselves defy and hate their own mothers. The mother of Elaine, the 14-month-old girl from Dr. Galenson's low-income high-risk family program, is a good example of this attitude (Galenson, Chapter 4, this volume). Because babies are bad by nature, the only parenting that is really needed is moral training, and physical punishment is the rule.

Clinical research has shown that as one goes up the at-risk ladder, words of angry criticism become the only ones a mother speaks to her child, while words of love or encouragement disappear altogether. I have been in rooms filled with a dozen and a half of our more dysfunctional mother–toddler pairs and have not seen one smile nor heard one laugh. The mothers cluster in a corner talking to one another, often eating and refusing to share the food with their children. The children run around the room engaged in mindless destructive activities, strewing wreckage wherever they go; they are oblivious to their mothers' orders to stop or be quiet, yelled at them from a distance. Dr. Galenson observed this kind of interaction between Elaine and her mother (Galenson, Chapter 4, this volume).

For some of us, this is a frightening and depressing scene to witness. For the grandmothers who teach this style of child rearing and their adolescent mother pupils, this way is right. This is not a matter of simple misinformation that some teaching can correct; it is a community-based belief system and a part of the character structure of each individual. They resisted being taught what we viewed as more growth-promoting child-rearing practices. For instance, a so-called preventative program was attempted in which workers brought toys to the homes of some of these young mothers and instructed them how to use them to play with their children. The toys were carefully selected to be age appropriate, and the worker visited weekly, each time with a new toy. We found that most mothers put the toys away, often on the top shelf of a closet, thinking that the idea of playing with their child was silly. All too often they simply smiled knowingly at the worker's efforts to teach them how to stimulate their infants, even when doing so would bring a limp and vacantly staring infant to life; again, they knew better. What they knew was the right way to rear children who were narcissistically damaged, related aggressively rather than libidinally, and were ineducable and violent—characteristics that I found typified the more damaged children who had grown up within this system of maternal deprivation. As adolescents, these children are prone to have children whom they will rear according to the same beliefs. Dr. Galenson's case of Larry, the failure-to-thrive baby, is a good example of generational maternal deprivation (Galenson, Chapter 4, this volume). Cultures perpetuate themselves.

Winnicott said there is no such thing as an infant (Winnicott 1960). He meant that without a facilitating environment—a mother—an infant cannot survive. Freud said, similarly, that a mother and her infant form a single psychical unit (Freud 1911). To some extent one can also say that there is no such thing as a family, that a family lives within a particular community, with its particular values and belief systems. Just as a parent acts as an ego auxiliary for the child, so does the community act as an ego auxiliary for the family, offering its mores as an organizing guide for the family members in their interactions with each other and with their neighbors. It is in keeping with that role that community-based rituals exist for such activities as betrothal, marriage, birth, and child rearing. As with Dr. Galenson's case of Maude, one sees the signs and symptoms of maternal deprivation in the affluent neighborhoods from which we draw our private child and adolescent patients, but they are nevertheless somewhat different from the inner city patients (Galenson, Chapter 4, this volume).

Dr. Galenson asks why there are such differences between her high-income and low-income patients: I think in part it is because in certain inner-city neighborhoods the system of beliefs supporting child-rearing practices based on deprivation is intimately enmeshed with the individual mother's tendency to deprive. In a community where maternal nurturance is the ideal, to some extent the community can help to offset the impact of one mother's personal inadequacies by promulgating its values through such communal activities as social gatherings, school meetings, church and synagogue activities, and even exchanges over the backyard fence. Changing a community's belief systems is a formidable task, but throughout history, spontaneous changes in child-rearing practices have probably been the most effective and least controversial way that this has occurred. The hope of parenting education is to reverse the direction of the self-perpetuating cycle: If children within this system can be reared differently, certain characteristics in adulthood—in this instance, the tendency to maternal deprivation—will change.

It is not surprising that our parent training program worked best when the mother developed a positive, dependent, mentor-like relationship with her worker and the agency, and could experience firsthand a nurturant and self-enabling interaction. I suspect, for instance, that in those counseling sessions described by Dr. Egeland with his adolescent mothers, the fact that there was someone listening was more important than the actual content of their exchanges (Egeland, Chapter 2, this volume). These mothers were able to make the program into a new substitute community and ego-auxiliary, and would often come to the unit every day, even though funding regulations—which we ignored—did not permit it.

THE ABSENT FATHER AND THE DEVELOPMENT OF AGGRESSION

The factor that Dr. Galenson stresses as a possible explanation for the difference between her high-income and low-income cohorts is the absence of the father in the low-income, high-risk families (Galenson, Chapter 4, this volume). I agree with her observation that the absence of a father makes it difficult for the toddler to deal with his aggression. But I see it as describing a later phase in the process by which destructive aggression becomes a prominent characteristic in low-income and depriving families (Burland 1986).

Dr. Galenson quotes McDevitt as saying psychological structure formation in the context of object relations begins in the very first months of life, a fact by now well established. In the low-income, high-risk, one-parent households under discussion, the lack of a marital or even conjugal relationship between the biological parents is itself an expression of a deeper problem with interpersonal relationships that impacts upon the mother–infant interaction from the start. A recognizable developmental pattern became evident, especially in the more dysfunctional mother–infant pairs. During their pregnancy, the mothers related to their unborn babies in an aggressive manner, hating them or expecting the worst of them. Although concern has been expressed that inadequate prenatal care is largely to blame for the poor health statistics among high-risk infants, the pediatrician who was a consultant to our program told me that many of these babies in fact are born healthy, but go down hill after birth due to poor maternal care.

As a consequence of these very early failures on the part of the mother to libidinally invest her infant, the infants do not, in Spitz's term, establish a libidinal object (Spitz 1965). Because their first internal object forms around unpleasure rather than pleasure, it might be said that they establish instead an aggressive object, a step in the development of the protosadomasochism of which Dr. Galenson spoke. One sees this reflected in the use of auto-aggression for self-soothing so common in these children. I recall one young foster child who put himself to sleep by banging his head against the bed frame so violently that he had permanent scars on his head and kept breaking the bed frame. One can only speculate on his early history and internal object relationships that evoke his infantile dyadic partner by such self-mutilation. Without an adequate libidinal object to act as a beacon, development is skewed, especially in all ego skills related to socialization. Self-reliant skills like walking develop early, allowing control of the distance from the aggressive object. But speech, for instance, is almost always delayed, as there is little sense of a libidinal object with which to communicate. Hatching is abortive, so that these children are not perceptually or cognitively well related to reality. They gather only limited information about the real world, most of it related to survival techniques, and remain perceptually egocentric, primarily responsive to their inner states, moods, and needs. Because of the preponderance of aggressive introjects, relationships are primarily perceived and experienced as hostile, exploitative, and predatory, and mood and imagery are predominantly angry. One can hypothesize and even occasionally get a glimpse of a deep and profound underlying anaclytic depression hiding behind the defensive malevolent hypomania.

I often wondered what became of the children's libido; we saw so little evidence of it directed toward external objects. What I concluded was that it was directed toward internal templates on the average, expectable, good-enough mother that infants are prewired to seek and interact with. Masud Khan suggested that schizoid characters relate libidinally only to split off and sequestered internal images of the ideal mother (Khan 1960); in fact, the descriptive label *schizoid,* as used by the English object-relations school, is appropriate for these children (Kohon 1986).

Dr. Galenson cites Meers's work with ghetto children: I interpret my similar data differently than he does. He refers to the ubiquity of sexual traumata among children in the ghetto (Galenson, Chapter 4, this volume). First, I am not sure that the sexual experiences described were truly traumatic or if the traumatic element of the sexual activities was sexual at all. There is a great deal of sexual behavior among these children, almost all of it promiscuous—that is, not visibly object related—and polymorphous. A seven-year-old inner-city boy I saw in analysis for three-and-a-half years masturbated openly and frequently, and engaged in oral, anal, and genital sex with the other boys and girls at the residential facility at which they lived. His masturbatory fantasies were violent and grandiose. In his play, for instance, dollhouse figures or hand puppets engaged in intercourse, but instead of loving cooing, the dolls argued angrily during intercourse. Their yelling and screaming grew louder, the pelvic thrusting grew more and more violent, the boy smashed the girl so hard she flew across the room and fell to the floor, and my patient stomped on her, laughing with malevolent and grandiose glee. In the accompanying affect, which was intense, as well as in the content of the play, the aggressive element far outweighed the erotic. As to the developmental importance of masturbation, a point Meers and Dr. Galenson underscore, when it is accompanied by object-related, primarily libidinal fantasies, it plays a very important role, especially in adolescence. But in this high-risk population, the mechanical act of genital manipulation seems instead to be psychologically related to a stalled and skewed developmental pattern.

By the time the children have reached rapprochement, the hostile introjects so outweigh the positive, in many instances there is almost no way the split in the relationship with the mother can be healed. There is little motivation to do so since there is not enough loving introject to preserve. As Dr. Galenson points out, the presence of a father would help in the healing of the split, so important to the resolution of the rappochement developmental challenges. By father I mean a psychological father, with a significant affective presence in the lives of both child and mother. In many of these families the absence of such a psychological father is a symptom of the problem in the first place.

This is best conceptualized from the perspective of object relationships. Freud discovered the power of our instinctual drives in our daily functioning, but also in our development. Although he recognized that drives are directed toward objects, he remained wedded to a view of the human psyche from a drive perspective. Infant research—especially the work of Margaret Mahler—has taught us that relationships with primary objects are developmentally more important than the mere gratification of drives, even though drives energize much of that interaction (Mahler et al. 1975). Here, too, I would interpret my data from the inner city differently from Meers. He seems to take a drive-related perspective and assumes that behaviors that lead to sexual arousal and orgasm are best understood as expressions of libidinal drive activity. In this population, when one examines the nature of the investments in internal and external objects, the object-aggressive and narcissistic-grandiose elements seem far more prominent than the libidinal ones. I agree that there are problems with sexual identity in this population, but I see it as related to poor differentiation between self and object, and the multiplicity of split-off, sequestered, primarily aggressive and narcissistic part-objects and part-selves.

Our years of research have helped us understand in ever greater depth how the primary objects—the parents—maximize their childrens' psychological development and well-being. Dr. Galenson's work with at-risk children would not have been possible without our insights into what good-enough parenting should be, and how children tell us through their problems in development what went wrong with their parenting. In fact, her own body of research has itself been the source of much of what we know about childhood development. Put in nontechnical language, the best preventative measure our years of research and study have come up with is that infants need parents. This is a conclusion that seems so self-evident it brings to mind Freud's oft-quoted, wry remark that with his theory of infantile sexuality he discovered what nursemaids always knew.

WILL THERE EVER BE PREVENTION IN MENTAL HEALTH?

Dr. Galenson states that there is a great need for remedial attention for vast populations of at-risk children, particularly within low-income, high-risk families. That means we need the mental health personnel to do the job, and that it is up to us to devise the curricula for their training, using the knowledge accumulated through years of research. I completely agree. But from what I saw in a dozen years in a few neighborhoods of one city, the scope of the problem on a national—let alone international—scale is overwhelming. The number of potential patients runs into the millions. Further, mental health intervention is labor intensive. It takes hours and hours of individual attention to bring about significant changes in the way the mind works.

The skills needed to effect such changes are great and complex, not the least of which involves learning how to cope with the intense transference–countertransference enactments such resistant and hard-to-reach clients provoke. This means developing a capacity for self-observation and self-analysis, skills that are not easily taught or learned. As a psychoanalyst I believe that a sensitive and attuned therapeutic relationship over time is the best way to obtain a true measure of a young mother's functioning, but it is far from easy to master such clinical skills.

There is a variety of high- and low-income, multirisk families requiring a sophisticated therapeutic flexibility; program approaches must be tailored to the needs of each situation, which requires more than learning intervention techniques by rote.

There are a variety of programs for the different populations, each with a varying degree of effectiveness. We all ache when we see a dysfunctional mother–infant dyad or a failure-to-thrive child, and the urge to eradicate such unnatural and inhuman pain from the face of the earth is understandable. I am reminded of an adolescent I had in analysis who was aghast at learning of the number of poor and destitute families in the world. One night he tried to conceptualize all the suffering of all the people in the world, and he collapsed to the floor in despair; literally he fell to the floor. I often recall his experiment and think of the mental work we all must do to spare ourselves a similar response when we are reminded of the extent of human psychological misery.

Perhaps now when we ask if there will ever be prevention in mental health, we can answer positively, thanks to individuals who are included in innovative and experimental programs like those of Dr. Galenson and her colleagues. We are contributors to, participants in, and observers of a natural evolutionary experiment: the human animal. In spite of an inherent resilience, humanity's many vulnerabilities must make us wonder how successful that experiment will be.

REFERENCES

Burland, J. A. (1984). Dysfunctional parenthood in a deprived population. In *Parenthood: A Psychodynamic Perspective,* ed. by R. Cohen, B. Cohler, and W. Weissman, pp. 148–163. New York: Guilford.

——— (1986). The vicissitudes of maternal deprivation. In *Self and Object Constancy: Clinical and Theoretical Perspectives,* ed. R. Lax, S. Bach, and J. A. Burland, pp. 324–347. New York: Guilford.

Freud, S. (1911). Formulations on the two principles of mental functioning. *Standard Edition* 12:213–226.

Mahler, M., Pine, F., and Bergman, A. (1975). *The Psychological Birth of the Human Infant.* New York: Basic Books.

Khan, M. M. R. (1960). Clinical aspects of the schizoid personality: affects and techniques. *International Journal of Psycho-Analysis* 41:430–437.

Kohon, G., ed. (1986). *The British School of Psychoanalysis: The Independent Tradition.* London: Free Association Books.

Spitz, R. (1965). *The First Year of Life.* New York: International Universities Press.

Winnicott, D. W. (1960). The theory of the parent–infant relationship. In *The Maturational Processes and the Facilitating Environment,* pp. 37–55. New York: International Universities Press.

6

DOES PREVENTION IN MENTAL HEALTH MAKE SENSE?

Henri Parens, M.D.

We live in an era in which some would argue against the feasibility of prevention in mental health by means of psychodynamically based intervention or by parenting education strategies that can lead to growth-promoting rather than growth-disturbing parenting. A major dispute comes from the conflicting assumptions that early childhood experiences do not leave evidence of their influence in later life (Kagan 1984), that inborn, biological dispositions are the sole determiner of personality formation, and that early life experience plays no part in this formation (Bridger 1989). If these assumptions are right—if soma and psyche are independent entities with no reciprocity, if nature is all-determining and nurture is impotent—this volume should not be put in print. On the other hand, if I can present data from neuroscience and propose some powerful postulates that reject the above disclaimers, then this volume should be printed and may be of help.

THE COMPLEMENTARITY OF INBORN DISPOSITIONS AND EXPERIENCE

I assert, as have many since Freud (Freedman 1992, Gabbard 1992, Kandel 1979, 1991), that mental health development and adaptation are codetermined and influenced by both inborn dispositions and experience. Regarding evidence of inborn dispositions, I have seen patterns of reactivity in newborns that give evidence of more or less organized ways of reacting. In the children we observed twice weekly from the first weeks of life to age 4 to 5 years, I found the same specific patterns of reacting to variable experiences to be evident over time (Parens 1979, Parens et al. 1993). McDevitt (1991), an original member of the Margaret Mahler research group, reports and details the same finding based on some twenty years follow-up of children seen several hours weekly for the first several years of life. We learned to predict how specific infants would react in given situations from early on. Cindy, the younger of twins, predictably had a short lag period before she quickly and sharply expressed distress. From the first weeks of life, her twin, Candy by contrast, could be relied upon to wait without undue distress for mother to tend to her. There were some surprises, but none very dramatic. For instance, two of our seventeen infants were quite calm and subdued from birth through the first 6 months. During the 8 to 11 month period, they became notably more motorically active than before and explored more vigorously than we would have predicted. They shifted from a previously recorded low activity type to a high activity type (Alpert et al. 1956, Bergman and Escalona 1949).

Although these inborn reactivity patterns showed stability, they could be influenced by the mother's reaction to the children. Cindy was made to suffer less because her mother, with our help, came to recognize Cindy's built-in low threshold for irritability, which could be mitigated by mother's soothing and comforting. As a result, Cindy did not become enraged or painfully disorganized, nor did she need to use early self-protective operations (defenses) such as withdrawal or contact (or gaze) avoidance. To the contrary, she welcomed her mother's caregiving, soothed and calmed readily, and developed, as did her older twin, a loving, secure attachment and basic trust, despite her inborn vulnerabilities.

Although at Cindy's birth we could not modify or improve the status of her central nervous system diatheses, we could help to optimize her mother's reactions to her and thereby, as we later observed and documented, facilitate secure relationships with her mother, father, and siblings, as well as her adaptation. (Cindy further benefited from dynamic psychotherapy during her elementary school years when she was stressed and struggled both in school and at home due to inborn perceptual problems, which were recognized very early. She is now in college and doing well.) (Parens et al. 1993).

Borrowing from the powerful model from biogenetics, no doubt this genotype could have evolved into a quite different phenotype. She could easily have become a person much less well related, much less emotionally healthy, and much less well adapted in life; in fact, she is a bright, attractive, loving, and good humored young woman, as is her twin (Parens et al. 1993). To be sure, in longitudinal research we cannot too firmly assert as I just have that this child could easily have become much less well related, healthy, and adapted. We cannot rerun her life under different conditions and, as many of us have gathered from empirical work, we cannot find a control outside of her who would meet even the major parameters of her inborn dispositions. Nonetheless, my assertion is common sense and one acceptable on the basis of consensual validation coming from nearly a century of clinical work and decades of direct observational research.

Arguments for and against the assertion that experience and inborn dispositions are codeterminers of the outcome person (phenotype) continue to this day. Some prominent biological psychiatrists (e.g., Wagner Bridger, in his 1989 Presidential Lecture to the Society of Biological Psychiatry) and extremists of discontinuity theory (Kagan 1984) assert that the influence of experience on the early patterning of modes of adaptation is not continued for life, that past adaptations do not dictate future ones nor influence new developments.

The other side of the debate is argued by different findings. Recognizing that discontinuity theory's argument lies primarily in the fact that symptomatic expressions of emotional problems change over the course of development—a factor recognized by psychoanalysts for decades (A. Freud 1965)—Sander (1985) has proposed that continuity in clinical symptoms is not the place to look for developmental continuity but rather, that it is in the domain of *patterns of adaptation* (i.e., in ego functions and therewith superego functions and id expressions). It is here that developmental continuity is found, not simply in the symptomatic ways maladaptive functioning may be expressed.

The development of patterns of adaptation has long preoccupied psychoanalysts, stated especially in terms of psychic structure formation. From Freud's cardinal assumptions that the ego and the superego are the precipitates of past object relations (1923), that the child bears the stamp of these relationships (1939), through Hartmann's revisions of the genesis of the ego as the organ of adaptation (1939), psychoanalysis has been on a course to conceptualize the development of psychic structure. The gradual process of psychic structure formation by means of introjections and identifications—which correlate closely to Piaget's concepts of assimilation and accommodation—and much theorizing about its intimate links to psychic representation (Novey 1958, Parens 1970, Sandler and Rosenblatt 1962) have been at the center of psychoanalytic theorizing and explorations in clinical work. Kernberg's (1966) hypothesis that experience is internalized in units of self-object-affect, complemented by G. Klein's Piaget-derived propositions recently elaborated by Slap and Slap (1991) on the structuring of internal representation in schemas of increasing complexity, elaborate existing theory on the development of increasingly stabilizing patterns of adaptation.

We can now add as well, from recent psychoanalytic observational research, the hypothesis that patterns of adaptation and psychic structure formation occur as a result of the internalization of experiential episodes or events (Parens et al. 1986, 1989, Settlage et al. 1985, Stern 1985). Stern points to the influence of repetition as setting down patterns (or schemas) of experiencing and reactivity that achieve stability. He points out, however, that unexpected experience also impacts on the self and, depending on its qualitative parameters, may become schematized by virtue of its unexpectability, especially when the experience has a traumatic influence. My colleagues and I (Parens et al. 1989) have proposed that early experiences of hostile and hateful parent–child interactions become internalized in episodes and progressively lay down patterns of reactivity that stabilize and codetermine the development of aggression (hostile destructive and nondestructive) in the child. Similarly, Settlage and his colleagues have pointed to the patterning of the infant's appeal for help to the mother under conditions of stress, noting the influence of the mother's reactivities as part of what the child internalizes, in episodes they have labeled the appeal cycle. From Freud on, psychoanalysts have assumed that experiences that create painful, dysphoric affects become emotionally invested and intrapsychically stabilized perhaps even more readily than do neutral or gratifying experiences.

Like Weil (1985), I have long assumed that psychic structure formation and patterns of adaptation have correlates beginning in earliest life in structure formation of the central nervous system. In 1985 Weil observed: ". . . that experiences induce neurophysiological structuring is increasingly recognized and traced into even finer areas. . . . Could it be that because *neurophysiologic* structuring is involved, this symptomatology [which she found in two adult patients the origins of which she reconstructed to the first two years of their lives] is so pervasive and so persistent?" (1985, pp. 336–337).

FINDINGS FROM NEUROBIOLOGY

We find support for this thesis in a number of neuroscience publications. In fact, Meyersburg and Post (1979) have gone so far as to propose a neurobiologic-psychoanalytic integration. Meyersburg and Post postulate that

> during the early months the striatic and limbic systems subserve the task of integrating and storing emotional and perceptual experiences. Severely painful emotional loading of early experiences may establish memories which have disruptive potentialities not only by facilitating disphoric responses to a repetition of the early stimuli but possibly by exerting . . . *influence on the subsequent development and maturation of neural structure. . . .* The memories of these experiences will replicate the disphoric tone of the primary episode as well as the general state of being which prevailed at that time. . . . If disphoric experiences are too intense, correspondingly intense memory processes evolving in the limbic substrates may remain inadequately modulated by higher neocortical centers and may evolve into autonomous excitational foci. [pp. 144–145; my italics].

The authors propose that there are critical periods for neuronal development and that "trauma occurring during a vulnerable period may evoke aberrant neuronal development and may leave permanent effects on neuro-organization" (p. 150).

In their book on *Child Neuropsychology,* Rourke and colleagues (1983) emphasize brain plasticity and assert that "the environment usually affects behavior." And they add: "It appears to influence the brain as well." They suggest that "the brain . . . is adaptative to the environment" (p. 101). They report on differential effects of social interaction (deprivation as well as overcrowding) on the chemistry and anatomy of the brain (p. 102), and conclude "that brain structure and function are not exclusively determined by genetic factors but that the environment is a powerful modifying agent" (p. 104). Indeed, they propose that "behavioral alteration, through psychologic manipulation, may alter brain function" (p. 107).

We have long awaited firmer neurobiological rather than consensual evidence coming from clinical and empirical work for documentation of the genetic assumption that it is *experience* that determines the specific phenotype out of the many but limited range any one genotype can yield. Ginsberg, a geneticist working on aggression, has the impression that given a vulnerable genotype, environmental conditions during sensitive periods of development will determine the outcome (1982). That experience is thought to critically impact on the organism during sensitive periods of development is also supported by many, including Kandel and colleagues (1991), Suomi (1982, 1991), and neuroanatomists Cunningham (1992) and Berman (1992).

When the brains of Harry Harlow's adult rhesus monkeys—those that had as infants been isolated with wire or cloth surrogate mothers (Harlow 1960, Harlow and Harlow 1962, Harlow et al. 1966)—were eventually examined, they were found to be markedly distorted by scattered massive cortical and subcortical atrophies. This finding gave rise to a debate about the factors responsible for these anomalies. Some asserted that emotional experiential factors played no role, that such atrophies—as well as the animals' behaviors—had resulted solely from a lack of motoric stimulation and activity and poor food intake. On the other hand, many assumed that while these factors played their part, reactions of loss and emotional deprivation and their aftereffects were putative as well (Suomi 1982, 1991).

Recent neurobiological work more firmly documents that experience determines the development of neuronal tracts, neuronal interconnectivity and circuitry, and functions to which they give rise (Berman 1992, Cunningham 1992, Kandel et al.

1991). We have long known that an infant born with a squint is at risk for developing blindness in one eye, amblyopia hemianopsia. This blindness is believed to result from the continued suppression of one image to eliminate the disturbing diplopia, causing suppression of retinal activity in that eye and atrophy of the optic nerve. We now know that it also impairs the visual cortex (Berman 1992). It is assumed now that the suppression or absence of function, that is, experience, leads to atrophy of the visual apparatus's underlying neurological structures in the central nervous system. In a review of pertinent studies Kandel and colleagues (1991) conclude that "Studies of the development of . . . ocular . . . dominance allow us to understand how . . . complex sensory experiences early in development may change the circuitry and structure of the growing brain." They propose that this results from interference "with activity-dependent development of neural connections" (p. 957) (also Berman 1992, Cunningham 1992).

Of course the function of the retina is crucial for the integrity of the optic nerve and visual cortex (Berman 1992); the function of the lower extremities is crucial for the integrity of the extrapyramidal tracts (Goldberger 1986); and very likely, the lack of physical stimulation and the highly restricted physical activity of Harlow's monkeys determined some of the physical and brain atrophies found after their death. But what about the influence of emotional and cognitive deprivational experiences? What about the influence on Harlow's monkeys of their separation from mother, their isolation from the group, their massive derailment of attachment, and lack of socioemotional stimulation and inhibition of physical and exploratory activity (Suomi 1982, 1991)? And what about their anaclitic depression (Spitz 1946) and withdrawal, and the inhibition in nutrition and motor activity characteristic of such emotional reactions? Animal scientists do in fact report physiological and neurochemical consequences to the emotional and cognitive deprivations experienced by monkeys experimentally tested as they were by Harlow

(Laudenslager et al. 1985, Suomi 1982, 1991). Indeed Kandel and colleagues (1991) find that "Studies in maternal deprivation provide a striking example of how genetic factors, development, and experience interact inextricably in early life and how environmental deprivation can dramatically alter [biological] developmental processes" (p. 957).

OTHER RECENT CONTRIBUTIONS FROM NEUROBIOLOGY

Firmer evidence helps us to assert that experiential factors are influential to anatomy, physiology, and neurochemistry of the soma, and specifically of the central nervous system. We now know, for instance, that stress impacts on the soma in a variety of ways. Decades ago, Selye noted its influence on the endocrine system. More recently, we have learned that stress, whether physical or psychological (usually both), impacts on the immune system by lowering the number of CD4-cells that perfuse the soma, thus decreasing the person's ability to fight the effects of pathogenic agents (Calabrese et al. 1987, Kiecolt-Glaser and Glaser 1986, Schleifer et al. 1985).

In the studies of a number of biological investigators including his own, R. M. Post (1992) finds documentation for a hypothesis central to my thesis. He postulates that sensitization to stressors and certain life events occurs and that these become encoded at a genetic level. Regarding the influence of psychosocial stressors on major affective disorders, he postulates that stresses and the biochemical concomitants of the episodes themselves "can induce the proto-oncogene c-fos and related transcription factors, which then affect the expression of [neuro] transmitters, receptors, and neuropeptides that alter responsivity in a long-lasting fashion" (p. 999). He observes that this new data from recent discoveries in neurobiology tells us how electrical and chemical stimulation and psychosocial stressors affect gene expression and allow an explanation whereby acute events can have long-lasting effects on subsequent reactivity of the organism. Post proposes that a similar type of process may occur in major affective illness as occurs in amygdala-kindled seizures. Following a series of stimulations, amygdala-kindled seizures eventually occur in response to a stimulation current that was previously subconvulsant, and, most important, that sufficient repetitions of full-blown seizures eventually result in the appearance of spontaneous epilepsy. In this model of amygdala-kindled seizures, there is a progression from seizures that are triggered by exogenous stimulation to ones that occur autonomously.

Developing his thesis soundly, Post notes that a number of investigators have demonstrated that even relatively common stresses are capable of inducing the proto-oncogene c-fos. A variety of neurochemical systems can induce c-fos; for example, water deprivation leads to increases in c-fos in the hypothalamus, or nociceptive stress so activates substrates in the spinal cord and other pain sites. He proposes that "the transient induction of c-fos and related transcription factors may . . . be an initial step in a cascade of neurobiological events" (p. 1002) that may have long-lasting effects.

Post elaborates how the induction of the c-fos proto-oncogene in turn induces mRNA, that "c-Fos protein is synthesized on the rhibosomes of the endoplasmic reticulum" (p. 1003), and that ultimately interlocking with another transcription factor, c-Jun, it binds to DNA. Post deduces then that "the oncogene 'milieu' *conditioned by prior experience* may markedly affect the subsequent alterations in gene transcription" (p. 1003; my italics). In this way responsiveness could be exquisitely regulated by *experience.* Post proposes that the repetition of stressors plays a critical role. Furthermore,

> the quality of the stressor may . . . affect specific neural systems based not only on the type and location of short-term biochemical changes but also on the type, location, mixture, and interac-

> tion of oncogenes and transcription factors, with differential consequences for subsequent coding of long-term protein and peptide changes. Psychosocial stressors involving losses and threats of losses in a social context may have very different cognitive, behavioral, and neurobiological consequences from other stresses. [p. 1004]

Let me conclude these considerations by turning again to Kandel and colleagues (1991). Reviewing cellular studies on synapse modulation and synapse formation, Kandel and colleagues (1991) propose that there are

> three overlapping developmental stages of synaptic modification. The first stage, synapse formation, occurs primarily in the early stages of development and is under the control of genetic and developmental processes, commonly cell-cell interaction. The second stage, the fine tuning of newly developed synapses, occurs during critical early periods of development and requires an appropriately patterned activity in neurons usually provided by *environmental stimulation.* The third stage, the regulation of both the transient and long-term effectiveness of synapses, occurs daily throughout later life and also is determined by *experience.* [p. 1028; my italics]

Kandel and colleagues (1991) propose that macrocellular structuring occurs by virtue of the effectance (activation) of activity-dependent cellular and intercellular mechanisms (also Berman 1992, Cunningham 1992). Thus, "*Environmental factors* and *learning* bring out specific capabilities by altering the effectiveness (and anatomical connections) of preexisting pathways" (Kandel et al. p. 1029). On the way to fulfilling one of Freud's hopes, Kandel and colleagues observe that "in the not too distant future we may begin to have a cellular neuropsychology of human mentation," including the capacity to explain the biological processes that underlie, or rather, that *are* complex ideas and feelings (p. 1029 [my italics]; see also Kandel 1989).

TOWARD THE PREVENTION OF EXPERIENCE-DERIVED EMOTIONAL DISORDERS

I have discussed Kandel's and Post's work to show that neurobiology is uncovering and documenting biological mechanisms that directly concern prevention in mental health, especially the prevention of *experience-derived emotional disorders* (in children). I have here detailed evidence from the neurobiological laboratories and clinics that validates the hypothesis that experience and inborn biogenetic dispositions are codeterminers of somatic structure formation and function. It furthermore gives validity (we are in fact coming close to hard and unequivocal proof) not only to continuity theory but also to the genetic point of view of psychoanalysis that early life experiences impact on the child's inborn dispositions to progressively organize patterns of adaptation (Sander 1985) and psychic structure formation that achieve stability—while retaining relative plasticity—as the child matures and develops (Hartmann 1950). The above named neurobiological investigators furthermore propose that the early years are a critical period for the earliest generation of postnatal setting down of activity-dependent (experience) brain interconnectivities and (phenotypic) synaptic fine tuning (Berman 1992, Cunningham 1992, Kandel et al. 1991, Meyersburg and Post 1979), for baseline experience-dependent genetic expression (Ginsberg 1982), and for baseline neurohormonal patterning of inborn dispositions (Landeslager et al. 1985, Suomi 1991). The critical periods factor is not absolute because these biological systems all continue to be variably and relatively experience-influenced as development continues into adult life (Berman 1992, Cunningham 1992, Calabrese et al. 1987, Kiecolt-Glaser and Glaser 1986, Post 1992). The plasticity of brain, hormonal, and other somatic systems has surprised many of us. Neuroanatomists-physiologists report a significantly greater plasticity (i.e., redundancy and complexity [Berman 1992]) in neuronal interconnectivity, which continues into adulthood, than has been heretofore assumed (Cunningham 1992, Rourke et al. 1983). From the perspective of clinical experience, psychoanalytic treatment has been shown to positively modify patterns of adaptation (although not of personality traits) where significant transference engagement occurred during the course of treatment—a critical but not surprising factor given the fundamental assumption that positive-enough, object-related experience is critical to positive adaptation (i.e., psychic structure formation) (Bachrach et al. 1991, Wallerstein 1986). I wonder, parenthetically, if problems found in some postpsychoanalysis follow up studies (Kantrowitz et al. 1990, Panel 1989, Wallerstein 1992) may in part be accounted for by the continuing experience-dependent somatophysiologic plasticity of soma that continues into adulthood.

In conclusion, we may assume that (1) biogenetic dispositions set inherent limits and characteristics of any human genotype; (2) experience forges these into patterns of adaptations, which achieve basic characteristics during the early years that acquire relative stability and form the foundation of personality; (3) ongoing development even into adulthood continues to be variably and relatively experience-dependent; and (4) experiences that have sufficiently powerful meaning to the individual can bring about modifications in even relatively stable somatobiologic systems and modify psychic adaptation (and structure), even when other personality factors remain invariable.

On the basis of these findings and postulates from the biological sciences, I argue that the better growth-promoting the early object-related experiences, the greater likelihood that the child will develop successful patterns of adaptation. These findings support the psychoanalytic genetic point of view, rejecting the conclusion that childhood experiences do not influence the formation of personality (Bridger 1989) and that these do not continue into adulthood (Kagan 1984). These findings and postulates also support the thesis of this volume: that we must develop strategies toward preventing the development of experience-derived emotional disorders and intervene early where evidence of maladaptation and mental ill-health appears.

REFERENCES

Alpert, A., Neubauer, P. B., and Weil, A. P. (1956). Unusual variation in drive endowment. *Psychoanalytic Study of the Child* 11:125–163. New York: International Universities Press.

Bachrach, H. M., Galatzer-Levy, R., Skolnikoff, A., and Waldron, S. Jr. (1991). On the efficacy of psychoanalysis. *Journal of thee American Psychoanalytic Association* 39:871–916.

Bergman, P., and Escalona, S. K. (1949). Unusual sensitivities in very young children. *Psychoanalytic Study of the Child* 3/4:333–352. New York: International Universities Press.

Berman, N. (1992). Personal communication.

Bridger, W. (1989). Child rearing and personality development: fact and fiction. Presidential address to the Society of Biological Psychiatry, May 4, San Francisco, CA.

Calabrese, J. R., Kling, M. A., and Gold, P. W. (1987). Alterations in immunocompetence during stress, bereavement, and depression: focus on neuroendocrine regulation. *American Journal of Psychiatry* 144:1123–1134.

Cunningham, T. (1992). Personal communication.

Freedman, D. A. (1992). Terms of engagement. Presented at the Winter meetings of the American Psychoanalytic Association, New York, December.

Freud, A. (1965). *Normality and Pathology in Childhood.* New York: International Universities Press.

Freud, S. (1923). The ego and the id. *Standard Edition* 19:3–66.

——— (1939). An outline of psycho-analysis. *Standard Edition* 23:141–207.

Gabbard, G. O. (1992). Psychodynamic psychiatry in the "Decade of the Brain." *American Journal of Psychiatry* 149:991–998.

Ginsburg, B. E. (1982). Genetic factors in aggressive behavior. *Psychoanalytic Inquiry* 2:53–75.

Goldberger, M. (1986). Personal communication.

Harlow, H. F. (1960). Primary affectional patterns in primates. *American Journal of Orthopsychiatry* 30:676–684.

Harlow, H. F., and Harlow, M. K. (1962). Social deprivation in monkeys. *Scientific American* 207:136–146.

Harlow, H. F., Harlow, M. K., Dodsworth, R. D., and Arling, G. L. (1966). Maternal behavior of rhesus monkeys deprived of mothering and peer associations in infancy. *Proceedings of the American Philosophical Society* 110:58–66.

Hartmann, H. (1939). *Ego Psychology and The Problems of Adaptation.* New York: International Universities Press.

——— (1950). Comments on the psychoanalytic theory of the ego. In *Essays on Ego Psychology,* pp. 113–141. New York: International Universities Press, 1964.

Kagan, J. (1984). *The Nature of the Child.* New York: Basic Books.

Kandel, E. R. (1979). Psychotherapy and the single synapse. *New England Journal of Medicine* 301:1028–1037.

_____ (1989). Genes, nerve cells, and the remembrance of things past. *Journal of Neuropsychiatry* 1:103–125.

Kandel, E. R., Schwartz, J. H., and Jessel, T. M. (1991). *Principles of Neural Science.* 3rd edition. New York: Elsevier.

Kantrowitz, J. L., Katz, A. L., and Paolitto, F. (1990). Follow-up of psychoanalysis five to ten years after termination: I. Stability of change. *Journal of the American Psychoanalytic Association* 38:471–496.

Kernberg, O. (1966). Structural derivatives of object relationships. *International Journal of Psycho-Analysis* 47:236–253.

Kiecolt-Glaser, J. K., and Glaser, R. (1986). Psychological influences on immunity. *Psychosomatics* 27:621–624.

Landenslager, M., Capitanio, J. P., and Reite, M. (1985). Possible effects of early separation experiences on subsequent immune function in adult macaque monkeys. *American Journal of Psychiatry* 142:862–864.

McDevitt, J. B. (1991). Contributions of separation-individuation theory to the understanding of psychopathology during the prelatency years. In *Beyond the Symbiotic Orbit: Advances in Separation-Individuation Theory,* ed. S. Akhtar and H. Parens, pp. 153–169. Hillsdale, NJ: Analytic Press.

Meyersburg, N. S., and Post, R. M. (1979). An holistic developmental view of neural and psychological processes: a neurobiologic psychoanalytic integration. *British Journal of Psychiatry* 135:139–155.

Novey, S. (1958). The meaning of the concept of mental representation of objects. *Psychoanalytic Quarterly* 27:57–79.

Panel (1989). Evaluation of outcome of psychoanalytic treatment: should follow-up by the analyst be part of the post-termination phase of analytic treatment? M. Johan, reporter. *Journal of the American Psychoanalytic Association* 37:813–822.

Parens, H. (1970). Inner sustainment: metapsychological considerations. *Psychoanalytic Quarterly* 39:223–239.

_____ (1979). *The Development of Aggression in Early Childhood.* Northvale, NJ: Jason Aronson.

Parens, H., Bockoven, D., and Goldberg-Moore, L. (1993). Follow-up study: effects of prevention/early intervention parent–child groups, a preliminary report. (Work in progress; see Chapter 7, this volume).

Parens, H., Singletary, S., Skivone, L., and Jessar, C. (1989). Toward preventing the development of excessive hostility in children: evolving methodology. Presented at the Mahler Research Colloqium in San Francisco, California, May 4, 1989; at the University of Philadelphia, February 15, 1990; and elsewhere.

Parens, H., Singletary, W., Skivone, L., et al. (1986). Toward preventing the development of excessive hostility in children. Presented to Research in Progress Seminar, Winter meetings of the American Psychoanalytic Association, New York, December 20.

Post, R. M. (1992). Transduction of psychosocial stress into the neurobiology of recurrent affective disorder. *American Journal of Psychiatry* 149:999–1010.

Rourke, B. P., Bakker, D. J., Fisk, J. L., and Strang, J. D. (1983). *Child Neuropsychology.* New York: Guilford.

Sander, L. W. (1985). Toward a logic of organization in psychobiological development. In *Biologic Response Styles: Clinical Implications,* ed. H. Klar and L. Siever, pp. 20–35. Washington, DC: American Psychiatric Press.

Sandler, J., and Rosenblatt, B. (1962). The concept of the representational world. *Psychoanalytic Study of the Child* 17:128–145. New York: International Universities Press.

Schleifer, S. J., Keller, S. E., Siris, S. G., et al. (1985). Depression and immunity. *Archives of General Psychiatry* 42:129–133.

Settlage, C. F., Afterman, J., Bemesdorfer, S., et al. (1985). The appeal cycle phenomenon in early mother–child interaction. Presented at meetings of the American Psychoanalytic Association, New York, December 20.

Slap, J. W., and Slap-Shelton, L. (1991). *The Schema in Clinical Psychoanalysis.* Hillsdale, NJ: Analytic Press.

Spitz, R. (1946). Anaclitic depression. *Psychoanalytic Study of the Child* 2:313–342. New York: International Universities Press.

Stern, D. (1985). *The Interpersonal World of the Infant.* New York: Basic Books.

Suomi, S. J. (1982). Abnormal behavior and animal models of psychopathology. In *Primate Behavior,* ed. J. L. Fobes and J. E. King, pp. 171–215. New York: Academic.

——— (1991). Early stress and adult emotional reactivity in rhesus monkeys. In *The Childhood Environment and Adult Disease.* Ciba Foundation Symposium 156:171–188.

Wallerstein, R. S. (1986). *Forty-two Lives in Treatment: A Study of Psychoanalysis and Psychotherapy.* New York: Guilford.

——— (1992). Followup in psychoanalysis: what happens to treatment gains? *Journal of the American Psychoanalytic Association* 40:665–690.

Weil, A. P. (1985). Thoughts about early pathology. *Journal of the American Psychoanalytic Association* 33:335–352.

7

TOWARD THE PREVENTION OF EXPERIENCE-DERIVED EMOTIONAL DISORDERS IN CHILDREN BY EDUCATION FOR PARENTING

Henri Parens, M.D.

INTRODUCTION

Prevention is not in the minds of most mental health professionals. If anything, the report prepared for The American Academy of Child and Adolescent Psychiatry by Shaffer and colleagues (1990) paints a gloomy picture for prevention, and tends to consider its application only to the most severe psychiatric conditions, mostly in the context of secondary prevention. Fortunately, there are a few who are not in accord with Shaffer and colleagues, who, like Berlin and Stone (1979), push to inform mental health professionals of the complex and multifaceted aspects of prevention in mental health, and encourage their engagement into prevention.

Interestingly, while the thought of prevention is equally far from the minds of most psychoanalysts (at least it is far from their writings), a number of child analysts have found themselves unavoidably staring at the obvious instances where our vast collective clinical experience informs us that treating a child one way will be growth disturbing and another way will be growth promoting. Clinician-researchers like Selma Fraiberg, Eleanor Galenson, Stanley Greenspan, Sally Provence, Calvin Settlage, and a handful of others have recognized with immediacy the many daily instances where principles of prevention can and should prevail. Child psychoanalysts are not alone in this experience. Benjamin Spock, T. Berry Brazelton, and other developmental pediatricians have also seen these daily instances and have pushed into the domain of prevention. Happily, developmental psychologists including Byron Egeland, Martha Erickson, and Alan Sroufe—especially those who include attachment theory in their work—have come to this point.

In 1933, Freud said that perhaps the greatest contribution of psychoanalysis would be its "application to . . . the upbringing of the next generation." He believed this contribution to be "so exceedingly important, so rich in hopes for the future" (p. 146). Our own work convinces us that what we learn by means of psychoanalytic observation—in both clinical and direct observational settings—can be applied to the upbringing of the next generation in a number of ways. In October 1978 I shared with Anna Freud some findings and plans for the education for parenting work; within days she replied: "I agree with you absolutely that psychoanalytic knowledge can be invaluable if brought to the public in this and other ways, and that at present, not enough is done about this" (A. Freud, personal communication, 1978).

How did we come to find ourselves squarely entrenched in this little-ventured-into domain and what are we doing?

HISTORY OF OUR PREVENTION PROJECT

In 1969 when we began attempting to correlate qualitative aspects of the child–mother relationship with the development of specific ego functions in the child, we did not know that some serendipitous findings would compel us into the study of prevention in mental health. Within two years of longitudinally observing mother–infant pairs in a group setting, meeting twice weekly with them for two-hour sessions, we discovered that we had found a method for parenting education (Parens 1988, Parens et al. 1974).

Prevention/early intervention mother–child groups consist of a group educational model for parents in which seven to ten mothers with their infants attend a 1½- to 2-hour weekly group meeting. The group meetings are instructed by psychodynamically knowledgeable mental health professionals. The instruction is not didactic; we do not give lectures. Rather, we discuss any issue that comes up spontaneously in this open parent–child group setting. The focus of our attention is the children's behaviors, with a view to talking about any issue pertinent to these behaviors found to be puzzling or troublesome to the mothers or the children. We also respond to questions the mothers have about dealing with children's behaviors and rearing. We emphasize that this approach is *educational,* guiding parents in their work (Fraiberg 1980, Fries 1946); but we also use skills we have learned from psychotherapy. We adhere primarily to *imparting information,* like instructors, because these mothers and children are not patients, but students. However, as is often necessary, we do borrow from supportive psychotherapy technique to enhance the parent's growth-promoting efforts and to facilitate the assimilation of information. Colleagues observing our work have repeatedly asserted that we are more than educational, that we are supportive, respecting, sensitive to the mothers' vulnerabilities, and encouraging of the parents' efforts in their parenting. We always search out a mother's growth-promoting parenting strengths; we always link the suggestion (with explanation why) for a specific change in any rearing issue with a related positive parenting function the mother has shown. Although we do not emphasize the psychotherapeutic aspect of this type of parenting group work, it is, nonetheless, similar to the therapy adjunct used by Fraiberg (1980), which she identified as *developmental guidance.*

We found that there is much factual information on matters essential to healthy child development that parents lack but is readily teachable. For example, we have often found gross misunderstanding of a child's emotional needs, of what will and will not spoil children, of what thumbsucking is about, of what transitional objects do for children, of what causes stranger anxiety and separation anxiety, of what the separation-individuation process achieves. Many parents know nothing about the Oedipus complex, what it does for and to children, how important it is to the development of morality, social conduct, and the ability to form good love relationships. Many parents do not know whether these ubiquitous phenomena are good, bad, or indifferent, nor do they know how to deal with undesirable as well as desirable elements in them.

Here are a few examples of the kind of phenomena I have in mind. From the time their children were about 6-months-old, two of the mothers would sneak out when they had to leave their children—say, for an appointment—in order to avoid upsetting their babies. They did not know that such disappearing acts—that is, leaving in a way that does not allow the child to become aware of the actual separation—at such a critical period of psychic immaturity, infantile omnipotence, and magical thinking can endanger the development of basic trust (Erikson 1959). Explanations of this matter were at first startling to these mothers, who had never been introduced to such ideas before. As is common, they found no cues to it in their own repressed childhood experiences.

Discussions of thumbsucking, separation anxiety, and stranger reactions took place frequently. Some of the mothers could not distinguish acute anxiety from (healthy) narcissistic orneriness. They did not know when to yield to their children's wishes, or when to frustrate benevolently. Too often they would gratify or frustrate at the wrong time. For example, when they are reprimanded by their mothers, 2-year-olds often become upset. When upset, the 2-year-old usually seeks comfort from the mother. Several good mothers rejected the child's request for comforting. Each mother felt that since the child had just been scolded, he was now trying to butter her up; thus, the mother concluded that comforting would spoil her child. These mothers agreed that the lesson would be defeated by the comforting.

The mothers did not know the error of that thinking and the harm that this approach can bring. Nor did the mothers know that comforting the scolded child can promote growth in two important ways. (1) Comforting can make the scolded child learn the lesson better because the admonition by the comforting mother tends to be internalized more readily than that of the rejecting mother. The influence of the comforting mother then becomes greater than that of the fantasied bad mother, whom the infant wishes to destroy. (2) Comforting the scolded child can ensure the fusion of good with frustrating mother representations, protect against splitting object and self-representations, and thereby secure a more advanced stage of object-relatedness and psychic development (Kernberg 1966, 1967, Mahler 1968, Mahler et al. 1975). Indeed, rejecting the child, especially under these conditions, reinforces the especially pathogenic defense of splitting by strengthening the influence of the bad-frustrating mother and bad self-representation. After a number of efforts at explaining these concepts, all but one of the mothers dealt with this matter quite well.

Discussion of children's interests in babies and their genitals was introduced by a 3½-year-old girl, who sent a shock wave through several of the mothers by announcing that she wanted to have a baby. Attaining conversational ease with sexual matters is a rather slow process. It is, in fact, the most difficult area for most of the mothers. By contrast, such areas as limit setting, ambivalence, hostility, and temper tantrums are much easier for them to discuss. Nonetheless, talking about sexual matters, when carefully dealt with, can be most beneficial. For example, one of our most skillful and talented mothers had a lovely relationship with her fifth child. Much warmth, compatibility, and comfort characterized their relationship. When Jane was about 2½-years-old, we began to see a significant change in their relationship; some of Jane's behavior led to considerable impatience, annoyance, and anger in this same good mother. Four months after we recorded this change in their relationship, the mother walked in and with a half-smile said: "Anyone want her for a year?" While this was said lightly, it was our cue to begin to explain that Jane was entering her oedipal period. We let Jane and the other children provide us with behavioral data from which we could illustrate, talk about, and gradually explain this salutary phenomenon to the parents. Because of the feelings stirred in the parents by their own children, they could readily recognize and appreciate this important, insufficiently discussed development. We observed—and the mothers confirmed our observations—that because the mothers could understand their children's behavior better, they could deal with it better. We also thought that they dealt with the behavior less conflictually. Education about the oedipal period is only one of many examples of increased parental comfort with sexual material.

We gradually came to recognize that our approach provides a method for educating mothers, fathers, and even children (Parens 1988, pp. 123–125). Our experience with families at substantial risk—though none were drug users there was some alcohol overuse—has been that the education-effected change in parenting quality began to show after about 18 months of twice-weekly group participation. Parenting changed from growth-disturbing to growth-promoting: on a ten-point scale parenting improved by 3.5 points (staff evaluations) to 5.4 (parent self-ratings), a substantial shift toward growth-promoting parenting.

By 1971 we encountered findings that challenged the then existing theory of aggression, and, abandoning our ego functions study, we began studying the development of aggression. We also studied the development of early gender formation in the girl. It is the aggression study especially that made us aware of the many episodes of child–mother interaction in which hostile destructiveness was instigated where it could equally readily have been mitigated. Similarly, we found many episodes in which nondestructive aggression (and the assertiveness and thrust to autonomy it fuels) was prohibited and burdened with conflict, when it could equally readily have been protected, sustained, and mediated with pleasure and rendered effective. Psychoanalysts have long assumed that these episodes become internalized, and as Piaget proposed by assimilation and accommodation, give psychic structure its characteristics (Kernberg 1966, Parens et al. 1982, 1989, Settlage et al. 1985, Stern 1985). This recognition, set in the context of 20th century history of Western civilization and present day social problems, thrust us into our interventional study "Toward Preventing the Development of Excessive Hostility in Children" (Parens et al. 1982, Parens et al. 1989). To achieve the goals for this study it became necessary for us to operationalize our mother–child interactional unit of observation, to develop interactional loci of observation (i.e., prototypic mother–child interactions), to develop strategies for educational intervention, and to develop an instrument for recording aggression activity in the child (the Excessive Unpleasure/Hostility Record [EUHR] [Giacomo and Parens 1982]), as well as two measures of parenting activity including a qualitative measure of their parenting functions in general (EPA Scale [Parens et al. 1986]) and of their parenting functions regarding the handling of their children's aggression (PCA Scale [Parens et al. 1987]).

As I said in *The Development of Aggression in Early Childhood* (1979), if the hypothesis that excessive unpleasure activates the generation of hostile destructiveness is valid, as our longitudinal research suggests, then we can find ways to prevent the development of excessive hostile destructiveness in children by educating caregivers including parents and child-tending professionals, to this finding.

FOLLOW-UP STUDY: PRELIMINARY REPORT

A 19-year follow-up study from the start of our prevention/early intervention project (reported in Parens 1979) has yielded the findings stated below (Parens et al. 1993). The original parenting educational project was conducted from 1970 to 1977; the details of the participants and the duration and frequency of their attendance to the program are reported in Parens (1979). The follow-up data were collected using several formats: (1) by means of mother and child questionnaires, which were followed (2) by one or two open-ended, semistructured interviews of each mother and each child. The mother's questionnaire consisted of two parts: (1) information about the child's development and history of mental health status, and (2) the mother's self-evaluations of her parenting functioning pre- and post-Prevention/Early Intervention Parent–Child Group experience. The original project observers matched the mothers' self-evaluations by their own blind (to the mothers' scorings) evaluations of the mothers' parenting pre and post group participation. In addition, the Fitzgibbons Anger Inventory (1984) was given to the children to ascertain the status of their anger and hostility. The following is a preliminary report of the follow-up findings. The larger part of this study, a collection of extensive case reports detailing the children's 19-year follow-up mental health status, is in progress.

The population consisted of seventeen children, thirteen girls and four boys. At the 19-year follow-up, five were under age 15. All families were from lower socioeconomic and lower middle socioeconomic groupings. Two of the children, one boy and one girl, were lost to the project by the one mother's withdrawal after one year's attendance. This mother's statistics are included in the change in parenting survey, implementing only the Early Child Development Program's staff rating. Parenthetically, it is the parents who were admitted to the program, not the children; as a result, our population of children was unselected and included one who was mentally retarded and suffered from cerebral palsy. Also, two permissions to interview were not granted by one parent, which disallowed our interviewing the children although they answered the questionnaire sent to them. On these two children the Fitzgibbons Anger Inventory was not obtained.

Our findings on this small group of subjects support the prediction that the educational parent–child group can produce significant, enduring benefits for both children and their parents. We feel these benefits are of major social value since they represent the development of productive, socially responsible young people, the majority of whom come from the lower socioeconomic group.

FINDINGS

General Adaptation Questions (Table 7–1)

Trouble with the Law: None of the youngsters was arrested or had other brushes with legal authorities. By contrast, in the population at large, there were 118.6 arrests per 1,000 among 14- to 17-year-old youths in the United States in 1985 (U. S. Department of Education 1988). In Philadelphia 21.4 percent of high school students were suspended at least once in 1986–1987 (*Philadelphia Inquirer* 1988a).

Drug Abuse: Of fifteen subjects, one used metamphetamine, which she reported to her parents and for which she went into drug rehabilitation. Parenthetically, this youngster was from the most troubled family in our group. The incidence,

Table 7–1. Prevention/Early Intervention Parent–Child Group 19-Year Follow-Up

Issues	ECDP	ECDP%	% For Population
Trouble with Law	0/15	0	14–17 Years (1985): 11.8% arrested
Drug Abuse	1/15	6.7%	Alcohol: Seniors: past 30 days: (1986) 65.3% Drugs: Seniors: past 30 days: (1986) 27.1%
School: Drop Out	1/15*	6.7%	8th Grade: 39% (2 sources)
Go to College	3/6	50%	20%
Teenage Pregnancy	2/12(15)+	16%(13%)	15–17 Yr. olds (1988): 10%
Parenthood	1/2(15)	8%(6%)	19 Yr. olds (1987): 10%

Population +17 children: 13 girls, 4 boys; 5 are <15; LSE & LMSE Population.
2 (1 boy & 1 girl) were lost to project by mother's withdrawal after 1 year; mother stats included in ECDP Staff Rating.
*1 Cerebral Palsy—mental retardation.

therefore, for the study group was 6.7 percent. With regard to the population at large, among U.S. high school seniors in 1986 any illicit drug use ever was reported at 57.6 percent. Any illicit drug use in the past 30 days was reported at 27.1 percent. Any alcohol use ever was reported at 91.3 percent. Alcohol use in the past 30 days was reported in 65.3 percent (U. S. Department of Education 1988).

Teenage Pregnancy (including boys' involvement): Two of the adolescents became pregnant. One pregnancy occurred in an 18-year-old and was terminated because it was tubal. Another 18-year-old had her second baby. Twelve of the subjects were 14-years-old and older; of these, two became pregnant, which records a 13 percent rate. The *Philadelphia Inquirer* (1988b), a local newspaper, reports that 10 percent of girls aged 15 to 17 become pregnant each year. Pregnancies among U.S. high school seniors were reported at 72.3 per 1,000 in 1983 (U. S. Department of Education 1988). Other reports suggest higher rates for community peers of the group we studied.

Teenage Parenthood (including boys' involvement): The 18-year-old woman with children attributes her pregnancies to the failure of birth control. This young woman felt regret that she had her children so young but reported that she would see to their needs first, and that she had implemented much of what she learned from her experience in the parenting group. Indeed, when this teen mother and her children were seen in several of our parenting group sessions, we found that her children were in quite good physical and mental health, appeared well cared for, and related very well to mother. When this young mother enrolled her 3-year-old in our therapeutic preschool nursery, the child was refused admission because he was too problem-free. Therefore, of the twelve youngsters over 14 years of age, one became a parent, yielding a 6 percent incidence. In the population at large, reports suggest a higher rate of parenthood in the population groups from which these youngsters come.

School Performance: One out of fifteen dropped out of high school, yielding an incidence of 6.7 percent. In the population at large, approximately 40 percent drop out of high school in the population from which these youngsters come. Except for the retarded child, who is in a training school for retarded children in which her progress is considered to be good, none of these children failed to achieve grade level work. Several of the younger children expressed interest in going to college.

Going on to College: Four of the 18-year-olds went on to college. One left college after one semester due to financial problems, but wishes to return. The other three are faring well in college. This yields three of six college age youngsters to be in college, an incidence of 50 percent. By contrast, in the population at large, 20 percent go on to college.

ANGER AND HOSTILITY

Hostility is our measure of problematic behavioral expressions of aggression (see Table 7–2). Our indices of hostility derive

Table 7–2. Prevention/Early Intervention Parent–Child Group 19-Year Follow-Up

Aggression

⋆FAI Parameters X	ECDP Aver. (n = 12)	FAI-Aver.
Anger	37.8	50.10
Trust/Mistrust	6.1	6.07
Passive Aggression	8.8	10.11
Violence Potential	5.1	7.96

⋆FAI = Fitzgibbons Anger Inventory
2 permissions to interview not granted by 1 father, FAI not available; 2 lost to project; 1 not applicable.

from the Fitzgibbons (1984) Anger Inventory (FAI), a questionnaire, which measures anger expressed in four modes: overall anger, violence potential, passive aggression, trust/mistrust. The FAI population scores are from a sample of adolescents in the community who scored with at least *moderate* manifestations of anger in the four modes. *Moderate* is considered a significant indication of potentially troublesome behavior, with deleterious consequences to the individual and/or others.

Overall anger: Our study group scored in the lowest category, *mild* anger. The community average for adolescents was *moderate* anger. The study group average was 37.8 (cut-off = 45); the urban population scored 50.1.

Violence potential: This score estimates the likelihood that excessive hostility may be expressed in violent actions toward others. The study group fell in the *mild* range, while the population at large slightly exceeded the cut-off, which indicates potential violent dangerousness. The study group score was 5.1 (cut-off = 7); the population at large scored 7.96.

Passive aggression: This category expresses the tendency of people to express anger only in indirect ways, sometimes with defiance, sometimes with self-defeating consequences. The study group is at the high end of the *mild* range, while the population at large falls within the *moderate* range. The study group registered an 8.8 score (cut-off = 9); the population at large scored an average of 10.11.

Trust/mistrust: Both study group population and the population at large scored at about the cut-off mark of 6.0.

CHANGES IN PARENTING

Changes in parenting were determined by assessments on four parameters considered of central importance in determining whether parenting is growth-promoting or growth-disturbing (Parens et al. 1986, 1987, 1989). Influenced by the parameters of the Evaluation of Parenting Activity Scale (Parens et al. 1986), the following measurements are used: (1) the mother's understanding of her child's behaviors and needs and the tasks of child rearing to optimize her parenting efforts and her child's development; (2) the shift in the balance of her loving and hating her child, which grows out of the mother's feeling her efforts to succeed/fail as manifest in her child's degrees of success/failure in development and adaptation; (3) the manifest and subjective feeling of her evolving effectiveness as a parent; and (4) the degree to which her functioning as a parent has contributed to her overall manifest and subjective feelings of self worth and competence as a parent and as an individual.

Two assessments were made; by the mothers, who rated themselves pre- and post-group participation, and by the Early Child Development Program staff, who participated in this work. The assessments are made on a 10 point scale (1 = least/worst, 10 = most/best), each figure representing the mean for the mothers as a group. Ten mothers participated in this group from 1 year and 4 months to 5 years and 6 months duration (average 4.4 years; median 4.1 years) for 1 to 4 hours weekly (average attendance was 79 percent). Of the ten mothers, eight rated themselves; despite several attempts, one mother did not return her self-assessment, and one could not be contacted.

The Early Child Development Program staff evaluated all ten mothers.

Table 7–3 represents the scores on changes in parenting. The results from the mothers' self-assessments indicate a rate of change toward better functioning of more than five points for each of the four parameters: 5.4 on understanding child and rearing, 5.2 on shift in ambivalence, 5.3 on effectiveness of parenting, and 5.6 on increase in feelings of self worth and competence. The range of change was from a pre-experience self-assessment mean of 3.3 to a post-experience assessment mean of 8.5+.

The results from the Early Child Development staff (there were four raters) are: changes of 3.9, 2.7, 3.8, and 3.8. The range of change was from a pre-experience assessment mean of 4.3 to a post-experience assessment mean of 7.7. Parenting can be expressed along the parameter of growth-promoting to growth-disturbing; if this is stated on a ten point scale, a change toward improvement in parenting of 3.5 (staff evaluation) to 5.4 (parent self-rating) can effect a significant shift toward growth-promoting parenting.

Table 7–3. Prevention/Early Intervention Parent–Child Group 19-Year Follow-Up

Changes in Parent Functioning

Change in Parenting Parameters (Means; 10 pt. Scale	Par. Self Ratings (n = 8*)			ECDP Staff (4) Ratings (n = 10)		
	Before	After	Diff.	Before	After	Diff.
Understanding Child & Rearing	3.2	8.6	5.4	3.4	7.3	3.9
Shift in Ambivalence	3.2	8.4	5.2	5.5	8.2	2.7
Effectiveness of Parenting	3.4	8.7	5.3	4.3	8.1	3.8
Self-worth and Competence	3.4	9.0	5.6	4.1	7.9	3.8

*One mother did not return self rating; 1 mother lost to project was included in staff evaluation (in project only one year; change minimal).

PARENTING EDUCATION FOR EMOTIONAL GROWTH: A CURRICULUM FOR STUDENTS IN GRADES K THRU TWELVE

While developing the project Toward Preventing the Development of Excessive Hostility in Children, we began to develop our Curriculum for Students in Grades K through Twelve, *Parenting Education for Emotional Growth* (Parens et al. 1993, work in progress). In 1976, the mental health team at Eastern Pennsylvania Psychiatric Institute (EPPI) (three child psychiatrists, three social workers, and three teachers) began to develop a curriculum for students in grades K through twelve. In 1977 we were joined by two teachers from the Germantown Friends School (GFS). From 1978 on we began a 9-year collaboration with educators at GFS, which included holding one of our weekly Prevention/Early Intervention Mother–Child Groups at GFS. We found that teaching these children about parenting was more feasible than we had anticipated. We knew from both observational and clinical work that these materials could be taught to elementary school-age children, a fact about which the teachers were initially skeptical. Buttressed by personal communications from Anna Freud in 1978 and from Margaret S. Mahler, we pushed through the EPPI turmoil of the early 1980s to continue to develop our curriculum. In the mid 1970s we found that educators at the national level were calling for parenting education courses for high school students (Parens 1988). During the early 1980s, understandably impatient with our slow pace and the complexity of our curriculum, several educators, led by Sally Scattergood at GFS, developed their own introductory curriculum, *Learning About Parenting* (Heath et al. 1983), which broke ground for parenting education in schools in Philadelphia and other cities. With much determination and a good deal of struggle, Education for Parenting—now under the directorship of Bonnie Raines—achieved their hard-won entry into public and private schools where they have been for a decade.

The mental health team continued to develop our parenting education for emotional growth curriculum. Having occasion to twice review and make recommendations to the teachers' introductory curriculum, *Learning About Parenting,* we became aware of a significant gap in reciprocal understanding of language and concepts that exists between mental health professionals and educators—a gap that over the years has substantially decreased. Nonetheless, anticipating a substantial degree of difficulty in preparing teachers to teach those elements of the curriculum we consider most likely to achieve our mental health prevention goals, we set out, under the leadership of Betty Scattergood, to develop our own lesson plans modeled after the teachers' *Learning About Parenting.*

WHAT IS OUR CURRICULUM?

There is much knowledge in the mental health field that is readily teachable to parents and young students. We have found that growth-promoting parenting can be greatly facilitated when the parent has a basic understanding of the complex nature of human development and can apply this knowledge to child rearing.

Our curriculum has several distinctive features:

1. It addresses the *mental health domain* of parenting. It consists of three subdomains of study: (a) human psychological-emotional development; (b) child rearing issues and methods; and (c) other pertinent parenthood issues.
2. The curriculum materials *start at the kindergarten level.* In a unique collaboration between mental health and educational professionals, these materials will be developed into a pyramid of grade-appropriate courses to span grade levels K through twelve.
3. This is a *laboratory type* curriculum. As in a biology or physics course, the students are exposed to live materi-

als, actual and specific child–parent interactional activities in the classroom as well as in outside assignments. Audio-visual materials are used secondarily to supplement live observations.

Parenting is a domain of information, knowledge, and skills that can be facilitated and enlarged by learning, much as is the case with reading, writing, arithmetic, biology, and so forth.

THE CURRICULUM

The basic contents of parenting education for emotional growth (Parens et al. 1993, work in progress) consists of a textbook or source book with model lesson plans drawn up at various grade levels corresponding to each issue detailed in the textbook.

The textbook is constructed as follows:

Parenting Education for Emotional Growth:
A Curriculum for Students in Grades K through Twelve

Introductory Unit A: Introduction to Parenting
Introductory Unit B: Pregnancy and Delivery
Unit 1: The First Year of Life
Unit 2: Years Two and Three (The Toddler Years)
Unit 3: From 3 to 6 Years (The Preschool Years)
Unit 4: From 6 to 10 (Elementary School Years)
Unit 5: From 10 to 13 (Pre-Adolescence)
Unit 6: From 13 to 21 (Adolescence, 3 phases)

Units 1 through 6 are structured similarly: each starts with a brief section on physical development, which pertains to mental life, namely, brain maturations that underlie new cognitive capabilities, or maturating pertaining to toileting training, or physical, hormonal changes that pertain to puberty.

In the section on psychological-emotional development, each unit is structured as follows:

Partial table of contents for Unit 2 (Years Two and Three):

2.1 Physical Development pertinent to emotional development
2.2 Psychological, Emotional Development
2.21 Adaptive, Part 1 (Ego Development)
2.2111 HD* Aspect of: Sleep-Wake Cycles
2.2112 CR* Aspect of: Sleep-Wake Cycles
2.2121 HD Aspects of: Affects
2.2122 CR Aspect of: Affects
2.2131 HD Aspect of: Cognitive Functioning
2.2132 CR Aspect of: Cognitive Functioning
2.22 Self and Relationships to Others (HD and CR Aspects)
2.23 Sexual-Reproductive Life (HD and CR Aspects)
2.24 Aggression (HD and CR Aspects)
2.25 Adaptive, Part 2 (Ego Development)
2.251 Dependence/Self Reliance (HD and CR Aspects)
2.252 Defense Mechanisms (HD and CR Aspects)
2.253 Empathy, Altruism, Sublimination (HD and CR Aspects)
2.26 Conscience Formation (HD and CR Aspects)

---

* HD = Human Development; CR = Child Rearing

The contents of each unit consists of *Issues*, each of which is continued through all the units, giving each Issue a developmental line. One issue pertains to affects, one to self and object relations, one to sexual-reproductive life, one to conscience formation, and so on.

Across the units, each Issue is addressed from the vantage point of child development, followed by a section from the vantage point of child rearing. Human Development states age-adequacy (A. Freud 1965) in capability and function. Child Rearing states growth-promoting, development-enhancing rearing rationales and strategies.

The following is an illustration of one issue in continuity through the units.

Self and Human Relationships Across the Units

Unit 1: *Attachment*

HD stated in terms of the theories of Spitz, Bowlby, and Erikson.

CR: Optimizing attachment with special attention to four attachment indices and basic trust.

Self and Human Relationships

HD stated in frame of separation-individuation (Mahler), Part 1: Symbiosis and Beginning Separation-Individuation; Hierarchy of earliest human relations.

CR: Optimizing the development of basic trust, symbiosis, and entry into separation-individuation.

Unit 2: *Self and Human Relationships*

HD stated in terms of separation-individuation (2nd and 3rd years).

CR: Optimizing practicing rapprochement, and on the way to constancy.

Hierarchy of Earliest Human Relationships

HD of relation to primary attachments (family) and to secondary attachments (nonparental caregivers).

CR: Optimizing both primary and secondary relationships (family and day care).

Unit 3: *Self and Human Relationships*

HD of self, differentiation of gender self.

HD of relationships: mother, father, including gender-based differences.

CR: Optimizing differentiation of gender self, and of these relationships.

(Stage is set in this section for the family romance detailed in the section on sexual reproductive life.)

Unit 4: *Self and Human Relationships*

HD: Status of primary and secondary relationships, role of extrafamilial relationships, adults, peers, one on one, and in groups. The special status of siblings (bridging peers).

CR: Optimizing these.

Unit 5: *Self and Human Relationships*

HD: Prepubertal self.

Relationships to parents, peers (siblings and others), other adults, idealized figures.

CR: Optimizing these.

Unit 6: *Self and Human Relationships* (three adolescence subphases: early, mid, and late-young adult; each subphase is addressed.)

HD: Status of self development, second gender self differentiation, ego-identity.

(Progression through three subphases)

HD: Relationships:

To parents—peers (nonfamilial)

(progressive shifts to the right through three subphases);

To siblings; peer relationships: Sexual and nonsexual, one on one and in groups.

To nonfamilial adults, idealized figures.

CR: Optimizing these.

A DILEMMA IN PARENTING EDUCATION FOR EMOTIONAL GROWTH

I find Unit 3 (3 to 6 years) the most challenging and problematic to bring to the public domain. The preoedipal era (separation-individuation, attachment, the development of aggression), latency, and adolescence are easy to teach.

The Oedipus complex is more difficult to bring to the public. Speaking of the sexual experiencing of 3- to 5-year-olds—which we have labeled the child's family romance—arouses much anxiety in many educators. We introduce this material gradually to parents when these behaviors appear in their children; parental resistance is lessened when this material is evident in the child and is sensitively addressed.

I have considered omitting this unit, but I find it impossible to address the preschool years without addressing the child's family romance. Such an omission would leave too great a gap because it would then be impossible to explain adequately the following developments: superego formation, the powerful impetus to neutralization of hostile destructiveness, consolidation of gender identification, altruism, empathy, and sublimation. All these are directly determined by the vibrant triadic conflict of ambivalence, the Oedipus complex. Unit 3 is essential for parents for the following reasons: (1) parents will more fully and sympathetically understand their children, (2) it may contribute to the prevention of sexual abuse of children, and (3) it may help prevent teenage pregnancy.

This textbook is almost sufficiently teacher-friendly. More work is required to facilitate its reading by nonmental health professionals. It can also be used as a source book for parents, day-care workers, parenting group instructors, and others. Teachers colleges might use such a text to form the basis for specialty education in parenting.

WHERE ARE WE HEADING?

The mental health team that developed Parenting Education for Emotional Growth jointly with Education for Parenting, the group of educators who developed the Learning About Parenting curriculum, are combining efforts to develop a demonstration program, the Parenting Education Middle School Initiative (PEMSI), which seeks to offer intensive parenting education to a middle school, grades 6 to 8, in Philadelphia. The overall mission of the project is (1) to teach parenting to middle school students who are not yet parents and to those who already are in order to better prepare them to be growth-promoting parents, (2) to develop a curriculum suitable for replication, and (3) to develop the context in which a longitudinal research project can be carried out. The curriculum from both groups will be integrated to provide the most feasible curriculum for the target school. The PEMSI project has two principal goals: (1) to provide all the students in the target school with a defined parenting education course; and (2) to develop a comprehensive parenting program for those students in the school who are already teen mothers. This comprehensive program will include our working in a parenting group with the teen mothers and their infants, and, where they are involved, the grandmothers. In addition, day-care services will be provided to the teen mothers so that they can continue their education; home visits will be made by professionals and monitored by our program; medical services for mothers and their infants will be provided within the school district.

The project will proceed in two phases. Phase 1, spanning a 3-year period, will give us an opportunity to integrate the PEMSI parenting curriculum and develop the necessary structure to carry out the comprehensive parenting program. During this period we will also research the effectiveness of the curriculum and prepare the way for carrying out phase 2 of this project.

Phase 2 will include the dissemination of the curriculum to other schools in the Philadelphia school district, reaching to grades below the 6th and above the 8th. The research plans projected for phase 2 are as follows:

Design: Upon conclusion of phase 1 of the program, the

teen mothers then enrolled in the target school will be matched by a comparison group in another Philadelphia school. A number of the services which will be provided for the target Philadelphia school mothers will also be provided for the other Philadelphia school mothers by virtue of existing community services (day care, social services, and medical services).

Predictions: Predictions will be evaluated in terms of short-term goals and long-term goals for both the mothers and for their children. During the school year, the short term goals are to help the mothers in the intervention program suffer lower rates than their control counterparts in (1) poor school performance and/or school dropout, (2) drug abuse and/or alcoholism, (3) child abuse, (4) failure-to-thrive infants, (5) repeat teen pregnancy, (6) HIV positivity, (7) mental illness (including depression and suicide). During these school years, the children of mothers in the intervention program will suffer fewer problems than the children of the control mothers in (1) attachment, (2) affect and mood, (3) aggression (heightened levels of hostile destructiveness, inhibitions in health assertiveness), (4) socialization, and (5) adaptation/mental health.

The long term goals (beyond the high school years) are to help the mothers who participated in the interaction program suffer lower rates than the control mothers of (1) below college-level education and/or no work training, (2) welfare dependency, (3) drug and/or alcohol abuse, (4) HIV positivity, (5) mental illness, (6) child foster placement, (7) child abuse. The children and adolescents of those mothers who participated in the program will have fewer problems than their control counterparts in (1) attachment and object relations, (2) aggression, (3) socialization and problems with the law, (4) school performance and continuation, (5) need for special education programs, (6) need for health treatment services, (7) teen pregnancy, and (8) drug and/or alcohol abuse.

Data Gathering Methods: Two interwoven investigative methods will be used:

1. Psychoanalytically derived data gathering methods, which will include (a) unstructured observations; (b) continuous observations with specific recordings every three weeks; (c) depth psychological inferences made from the data collection.

2. Developmental psychological methods, which will include (a) structured interviews and data gathering procedures (the Ainsworth Strange Situation, Sroufe and colleagues' problem solving situations) and (b) paper and pencil procedures (such as the Abidin Stress Parenting Index, Escalona Sensory Motor Development Scales, Achenbach and colleagues' System Check List) at predetermined times.

The composite of unstructured observations, structured observations, and paper and pencil procedures will allow us to access, by means of the measures employed, the data on the children, including attachment data, affect/mood, aggression, and the quality of parenting interventions derived from the measures of parenting activity.

Data Analysis: We assume that both group comparative studies and individual case studies will be done.

The aim of this chapter is to demonstrate support for the idea of prevention in mental health and its feasibility. To be sure, the project we have been working toward is complex and costly and will perhaps bear fruit mostly in the next generation. However, the issues at stake are enormous and we cannot afford to be timid in our efforts to remedy some of the most difficult problems we face both individually and as a society.

REFERENCES

Berlin, I. N., and Stone, L. A. (1979). *Prevention and Current Issues. The Basic Handbook of Child Psychiatry*. Vol. 4. New York: Basic Books.

Erikson, E. H. (1959). *Identity and the Life Cycle. Psychological Issues,* Monogr. 1. New York: International Universities Press.

Fitzgibbons, R. P. (1984). *Fitzgibbons Anger Inventory*. Bala Cynwyd, PA: Privately published.

Fraiberg, S. (1980). *Clinical Studies in Infant Mental Health: The First Year of Life*. New York: Basic Books.

Freud, A. (1965). *Normality and Pathology in Childhood.* New York: International Universities Press.

_____ (1978). Letter dated October 18, 1978. Personal communication.

Freud, S. (1933). New introductory lectures on psychoanalysis. *Standard Edition* 22:3–182.

Fries, M. (1946). The child's ego development and the training of adults in his environment. *Psychoanalytic Study of the Child* 2:85–112. New York: International Universities Press.

Giacomo, L., and Parens, H. (1982). Excessive unpleasure/hostility record. Final Report to the Fund for Psychoanalytic Research of The American Psychoanalytic Association, 1986.

Heath, H., Scattergood, S., and Meyer, S. (1983). *Learning About Parenting.* Philadelphia, PA: Education for Parenting (revised, 1988).

Kernberg, O. (1966). Structural derivatives of object relationships. *International Journal of Psycho-Analysis* 47:236–253.

_____ (1967). Borderline personality organization. *Journal of the American Psychoanalytic Association* 15:641–685.

Mahler, M. S. (1968). *On Human Symbiosis and the Vicissitudes of Individuation.* With M. Furer. New York: International Universities Press.

Mahler, M., Pine, F., and Bergman, A. (1975). *The Psychological Birth of the Human Infant.* New York: Basic Books.

Parens, H. (1979). *The Development of Aggression in Early Childhood.* New York: Jason Aronson.

_____ (1988). A psychoanalytic contribution toward rearing emotionally healthy children: education for parenting. In *New Concepts in Psychoanalytic Psychotherapy,* ed. J. M. Ross and W. A. Myers, pp. 120–138. Washington, DC: American Psychiatric Press.

Parens, H., Bockoven, D., and Goldberg-Moore, L. (1993). Follow-up study: effects of prevention/early intervention parent–child groups, a preliminary report. (Unpublished manuscript).

Parens, H., Giacomo, L., and McLeer, S. V. (1982). Toward preventing the development of excessive hostility in children. Presented at the meetings of the American Psychoanalytic Association, December 18, New York, NY.

Parens, H., Prall, R. C., and Pollock, L. (1974). *Prevention/Early Intervention Mother–Child Groups.* Film #3, Audio Visual Media, Eastern Pennsylvania Psychiatric Institute, Philadelphia, PA.

Parens, H., Scattergood, E., Duff, A., and Singletary, W. M. (1993). *Parenting Education for Emotional Growth: A Curriculum for Students in Grades K Through 12.* (Work in progress).

Parens, H., Singletary, W., Barcan, D., et al. (1986). Evaluation of parenting activity scale: development and reliability testing. (Unpublished manuscript.)

Parens, H., Singletary, W., and Jessar, G. (1987). Parents coping with their children's aggression scale. (Unpublished manuscript.)

Parens, H., Singletary, W., Skivone, L., and Jessar, G. (1989). Toward preventing the development of excessive hostility in children: evolving methodology. Presented at The Institute of the Pennsylvania Hospital, February 21, 1989; at Reading Hospital, April 25, 1989; at the Mahler Research Colloquium in San Francisco, California, May 4, 1989; and at the University of Pennsylvania, February 15, 1990.

Philadelphia Inquirer (1988a). News article. June 27, Section B, p. 7.

Philadelphia Inquirer (1988b). Special article. February 23, Section HS, p. 10.

Settlage, C. F., Afterman, J., Bemesdorfer, S., et al. (1985). The appeal cycle phenomenon in early mother–child interaction. Presented at meetings of the American Psychoanalytic Association, New York, December 20.

Shaffer, D., Philips, I., Enzer, N. B., and Anthony, V. Q. (1990). *Prevention in Child and Adolescent Psychiatry: The Reduction of Risk for Mental Disorders.* Washington, DC: American Academy of Child & Adolescent Psychiatry.

Stern, D. (1985). *The Interpersonal World of the Infant.* New York: Basic Books.

U. S. Department of Education (1988). (Office of Education Research and Improvement.) *Youth Indicators 1988: Trends in the Well-Being of American Youth.* Washington, DC: U. S. Government Printing Office.

8

EDUCATION FOR PARENTING

William M. Singletary, M.D.

In the final chapter of her *Memoirs* (Mahler 1988), Dr. Margaret Mahler's thoughts turn toward prevention and early intervention:

> If we can convey basic scientific understanding of the meaning of the rapprochement crisis to mothers and fathers, we will have taken an important step enroute to a strategy of prevention of childhood psychopathology. . . . To impart general knowledge of this sort is as important as to undertake further research aimed at refining our understanding of the process. And this is because education of parents subserves prevention and early intervention, which, to my mind, are the answers to major problems of our time. [pp. 151–152]

Clearly, Dr. Mahler felt that education for parenting is a natural outgrowth of psychoanalytic research in child development and can play a key role in prevention and early intervention. Her thoughts about the role of prevention in addressing our social problems are most timely. I will present some of the growing body of research supporting Dr. Mahler's beliefs. I will give a brief overview of some essential concepts in child development but focus mainly on education for parenting programs as well as comprehensive prevention programs and their cost effectiveness. I believe that knowledge of these effective programs can help to combat a pervasive sense of hopelessness and helplessness and can lead to a realistic optimism and to a determination to successfully confront our current social crisis.

KEY CONCEPTS IN CHILD DEVELOPMENT

We have many people to thank for the sound body of knowledge about human development and growth-promoting parenting that we use in education for parenting efforts. In addition to Dr. Mahler's (Mahler et al. 1975) separation-individuation theory, key contributions include Freud's (1905) psychosexual theory; Erikson's (1968) stages of development, which emphasize the importance of the establishment of basic trust along with a sense of autonomy in the earliest years of life; Spitz's (1965) formulations concerning the importance of the infant's attachment to primary objects; Bowlby's (1969, 1973) considerations of attachment, which added an ethological perspective and led to the crucial work of Ainsworth (Ainsworth et al. 1978) and of Sroufe and his colleagues (1982, Sroufe and Fleeson 1986) regarding the effects of the infant's developing a secure, as opposed to an insecure, attachment; Sander's (1983, 1985) studies of the mother–infant interaction and the process of development; Parens's (1979) work on the development of aggression in early childhood; Greenspan's (1981) work on developmental stages and the corresponding characteristics of the environment, which either serve to promote or to inhibit growth; and Stern's (1977) studies of the social interaction between infant and mother.

EDUCATION FOR PARENTING PROGRAMS

Two programs demonstrate that with this substantial body of knowledge, we can teach parents about human development and parenting and have a beneficial impact on parenting and on the child's development. However, we need individualized programs that begin either prenatally or at birth, involve both infant and parent, and teach parents specific ways to interact helpfully with their unique infant. First, the Missouri New Parents as Teachers project, based on Dr. Burton White's work and developed with his assistance, focused on first-time parents and served families on all socioeconomic levels. However, the evaluation focused on the less disadvantaged families (White 1988).

Although this program was designed to promote the development of new parents as their children's first teachers and was implemented in conjunction with the Missouri State Department of Education, its aim was to promote the general competence of the child (White 1988). From the third trimester of pregnancy until the child was three years old, families received a variety of services. Education for parenting was provided in regularly scheduled individual visits, usually at home, and in group meetings with other parents. The curriculum covered four major areas of development: language, curiosity, and intellectual and social development. It also covered ways parents could foster development in these areas as well as practical aspects of child rearing (Vartuli and Winter 1989). The attachment between infant and primary caregiver was considered to be the most important aspect of social development (White 1988). Until the child reached seven months of age, the central goal was to help the child achieve "a solid state of feeling loved and cared for" and "a healthy interest in exploring the environment" (White 1988, p. 167).

Other services included periodic screening of hearing, vision, and general development. Families were referred for special services as needed (White 1988). Evaluations done when the children were 3 years old indicated that program children scored significantly higher on all measures of intelligence, achievement, and language ability and demonstrated significantly more aspects of positive social development than children in a comparison group (Pfannenstiel and Seltzer 1985). Also, program parents were significantly more knowledgeable about child development and child rearing than parents in the comparison group (Pfannenstiel and Selzer 1985). White (1988) estimates that the yearly cost for a similar program would range from $700–$1,200 per family.

While the New Parents as Teachers program dealt with parents of normal infants, another program worked with parents of low birth weight infants. In reviewing studies of caregiver-focused programs for parents of premature infants, Seitz and Provence (1990) noted that greater parental sensitivity and better mother–child interactions have been consistently found in outcomes of these programs. One such program, The Mother–infant Transaction Program in Vermont (Rauh et al. 1988), attempted to improve maternal adaptation to the care of a low birth weight infant in order to facilitate infant development. In this program a nurse conducted eleven sessions with the mother both during the infant's hospitalization and over the first three months following discharge. The purpose of these sessions was to enable the mother to appreciate her baby's unique characteristics, to increase her sensitivity to her baby's cues, and to teach her to respond appropriately to these cues. For example, in the first session, the infant's potential for self-regulation and for interaction were demonstrated by using the Brazelton Neonatal Assessment Scale. In a seven-year outcome study, the authors concluded that their findings suggested that this program prevented cognitive lags by changing maternal attitudes and behavior and improving the quality of parenting (Achenbach et al. 1990).

COMPREHENSIVE PREVENTION PROGRAMS

Both of these were narrowly focused education for parenting programs. The role of education for parenting is one aspect of more comprehensive prevention programs. Before discussing specific programs, I will mention the findings of Lisbeth Schorr (1988) and present some thoughts about successful programs. In her compelling book, *Within Our Reach,* Schorr (1988) examines successful programs and demonstrates that now we are capable of dramatically reducing the incidence of teenage pregnancy, low birth weight infants, child abuse and neglect, school dropout, violent juvenile crime, adult criminality, unemployment, and welfare dependency. Schorr (1988) concludes that in order to be effective in addressing these critical social problems, programs must be intensive, individualized, and comprehensive (i.e., meeting multiple psychosocial and medical needs of parents and infants). She emphasizes the importance of a skilled, committed, caring staff who are able to form collaborative relationships with the people they serve. Schorr (1988) further concludes that such programs can be extremely cost effective. All of the comprehensive prevention programs that I will discuss had a component designed to enhance caregiver functioning. Each had some form of regular home visitation. In my opinion, the development of an emotionally meaningful relationship between the home visitor and the parents is an essential aspect of such programs. Furthermore, I agree with Seitz and Provence (1990), who suggest that fundamental principles guiding successful early intervention programs include the competence of the service provider, the continuity of care, and the formation of a working partnership between the service provider and the caregiver.

The Perry Preschool Program, begun in the early 1960s, had an experimental group of fifty-eight low-IQ, disadvantaged children, aged 3–4 years. Based on their IQs, many of the children could have been classified as mentally retarded (Barnett and Escobar 1990, Schweinhart and Weikart 1989). Most of the children participated in the program for two years. An educational approach based on Piaget's child development theory was used. The children attended the classroom program five days each week for seven months a year, and each parent was visited at home by a teacher once a week. Follow-up at age 19 indicated clear differences between the experimental group and the matched control group. The children who attended preschool were significantly more likely to have finished high school (67 percent vs. 49 percent), to be in vocational school or college (38 percent vs. 21 percent), and to be employed (59 percent vs. 32 percent). In addition, they were significantly less likely to be on welfare or to have been arrested (31 percent vs. 51 percent), and there were fewer pregnant teens (64/100 vs. 117/100, due to multiple pregnancies) (Berrueta-Clement et al. 1984, Schweinhart and Weikart 1989).

The Yale Child Welfare Program, carried out from 1967 to 1972 and directed by Dr. Sally Provence (Provence and Naylor 1983), involved seventeen impoverished women beginning during their first pregnancy. Each family received individualized supportive services provided by one consistent team including a home visitor (usually a social worker), primary day-care worker, developmental examiner, and pediatrician. These services were provided until the child was 2½ years old and included day care, regular home visitation, regular developmental examinations for the children, and pediatric care. The primary focus was on the emotional and social adjustment of the children and parents. The aim was to improve the parents' ability to care for their children and to solve their own problems in life. For example, day-care staff dealt with such child care issues as separation from the parents and helping the child learn to manage aggression (Seitz and Provence 1990). A ten-year follow-up study revealed considerable change in these families. Compared to a control group these mothers had fewer children, obtained significantly more education, and were significantly more likely to be employed and self-supporting. Their sons were much less likely to require expensive special services in the schools than were the control boys. In describing their classroom behavior, teachers rated control boys much more negatively (Seitz and Provence 1990). Control boys were much more likely to have problems with aggressive behavior both at school and at home (Seitz and Provence 1990). The parent–child relationships were clearly better in the intervention group than in the control group (Seitz and Provence 1990). This program fostered greater prenatal nurturance and strengthened the parent–child bond, which led to better emotional development and better social and school adjustment (Seitz et al. 1985).

The Prenatal/Early Infant Project was directed by Dr. David Olds and took place between the late 1970s and the mid-1980s. Involving 400 first-time mothers in a semirural area of New York State, the study actively recruited mothers who were either teenaged, single, or poor. The program was designed to prevent a range of maternal and child health problems such as low birth weight, child abuse, and neglect and to promote the health and well-being of both mother and child. For example, one focus was on the mother's own development, including reducing the number of subsequent pregnancies, completing her education, and finding work. Another focus was on improving the overall development of the child (Olds and Henderson 1989).

The visiting nurses had three major activities: parent education concerning influences on early development, enhancing the informal support available to the women through the involvement of family and friends, and connecting families with formal health and human services. Nurses worked to promote the child's physical health through parent education. They helped parents to understand the infant's temperament and used the Brazelton Neonatal Assessment Scale in their teaching. The nurses emphasized the infant's need for growth-promoting care, including responding to the infant's cues and communicating and playing with the infant; they responded helpfully to the older child's need for exploration and development of autonomy (Olds 1988). Olds (1988) stated, "Much time was spent helping parents understand their children's need for responsive caregivers whom they could learn to trust to respond to their needs" (p. 16). In other words, they worked to facilitate the formation of secure attachments (Olds and Henderson 1989).

The 216 families who received home visitation were compared to those who had not. Expectant mothers who smoked and were visited at home reduced the number of cigarettes smoked and had a 75 percent reduction in preterm delivery (Olds 1988). Compared to similar mothers who had never received home visits, the poor, unmarried teenagers who were visited at home until the child was two years of age had a 75 percent reduction in the incidence of child abuse and neglect (from 19 percent to 4 percent) (Olds 1988) and were observed to restrict and punish their children less frequently (Olds and Henderson 1989). In addition, during the second year of life, the children of women who were visited at home were seen in the emergency room 56 percent fewer times for accidents and ingestions (Olds 1988). The investigators suspected that the formation of secure attachments may have protected these children from abuse and neglect (Olds and Henderson 1989).

The Hawaii Healthy Start program began in 1985 as a demonstration child abuse and neglect prevention project and served 241 high-risk families. It has been remarkably successful, both in preventing child abuse and neglect and in expanding the state department of health (Breakey and Pratt 1991). By 1990, the program served approximately 52 percent of Hawaii's at-risk families of newborns (Breakey and Pratt 1991), and in a recent year, 3,500 families received home visitation services (Fuddy, unpublished). In addition to preventing child abuse and neglect, this program is designed to optimize child development by improving family coping skills, by promoting helpful parenting and helpful parent–child interactions, and by ensuring preventive health care (Breakey and Pratt 1991). Systematic hospital-based screening at the time of delivery is used to identify families at risk for child abuse and neglect. Paraprofessional home visitors provide support services as well as educational efforts aimed at improving parenting skills and quality of the parent–child interaction. Areas emphasized included teaching parents the importance of holding, talking to, consoling, and playing with the infant and helping the infant learn to trust and depend on the parents (Elliot et al. 1991). Another key component involves the coordination of health and social services with an emphasis on preventive health care. These services continue until the child is five years of age. Of the 241 families in the original three-year demonstration project, 176 had received services for at least one year at the time of the outcome assessment. At the end of the demonstration, there were no confirmed cases of abuse and only four confirmed cases of neglect (2 percent) of target children (Breakey and Pratt 1991). For 1,204 at-risk families who were involved in this expanded program in 1987 through 1989, there was only one confirmed case of child abuse (<1 percent) and only six confirmed cases of neglect (<1 percent) (Breakey and Pratt 1991).

A summary of the expected outcomes of such programs, for both the parents and the children, is provided in Figure 8–1. In developing this summary I have followed the lead of Seitz and Provence (1990) in their review article concerning caregiver-focused models of early intervention. In the absence of an existing ideal study, I have combined the findings of a number of studies to develop a summary of outcomes that could reasonably be expected.

COST EFFECTIVENESS

Both indirect costs (Eisenberg 1989) and indirect benefits (Barnett and Escobar 1990) make evaluating the cost effectiveness of

PARENTS: Improved/Increased

- ▲ Understanding of child development and rearing
- ▲ Parental sensitivity
- ▲ Quality of parenting
- ▲ Parent–child interactions and relationships
- ▲ Education
- ▲ Employment and self-support

Decreased

- ▲ Low birth weight infants
- ▲ Infant mortality
- ▲ Number of children
- ▲ Child abuse and neglect

CHILD: Improved/Increased

- ▲ Cognitive development
- ▲ Social development
- ▲ Education
- ▲ Employment

Decreased

- ▲ Aggressive behavior
- ▲ Problem behavior in school
- ▲ Need for special services in school
- ▲ Teen pregnancy
- ▲ Arrests
- ▲ Welfare

Figure 8–1. Expected Outcomes

prevention and early intervention programs a complicated enterprise. In discussing the cost–benefit analysis of the Perry Preschool Program, Barnett and Escobar (1990) point out that the costs were more accurately estimated than the benefits. In general, in such analyses of prevention and early intervention programs, some benefits, such as early IQ gains, increased school success and satisfaction, reduced teenage pregnancy, increased social competence in adulthood, increased sense of well-being in children and their parents, and increased feeling of safety in society at large due to reduced crime, cannot be valued economically (Barnett and Escobar 1990). However, there is now a substantial body of research indicating that early childhood prevention and intervention programs can be a sound investment (Barnett and Escobar 1990, *Children in Need* 1987, Greenspan 1982).

The Perry Preschool Program has been extensively studied (Barnett and Escobar 1990, Schweinhart and Weikart 1989). While the annual cost of this program was $5,000 per child (in 1981 dollars) or a total of $10,000 for the usual two years' participation, the total benefits to taxpayers were about $28,000 per child. This included savings per child of $5,000 for special education programs, $3,000 due to crime reduction, and $16,000 for welfare. There was an added college cost of $1,000 per child, but the average participant was expected to pay an additional $5,000 in taxes because of increased lifetime earnings (Schweinhart and Weikart 1989). The Yale Child Welfare Program cost $20,000 per family (in 1982 dollars) for a two-and-a-half year program or $8,000 per family for each year of the program. In a ten-year follow up Seitz (Seitz et al. 1985) found that the project seemed to be saving a total of $40,000 per year. Of this, $10,000 per year (or $1,000 per boy) was saved on special school services, while $30,000 per year was saved because the program families required less extrafamilial support. The authors concluded that, at that point, the program appeared to be paying itself off at the rate of two families per year (Seitz et al. 1985).

Olds (1988), while providing no figures for the Prenatal/Early Infant Project, indicated that preliminary analyses of cost effectiveness suggest that a major share of the cost for home visitation could be offset by savings due to fewer emergency room visits and hospitalizations, decreased need for child protective services, and fewer foster-care placements. He added that

DECREASED:
- ▲ Medical costs
- ▲ Special education
- ▲ Welfare for current parents
- ▲ Child protective services
- ▲ Foster care placement
- ▲ Crime
- ▲ Welfare for children as adults

Figure 8–2. Expected Economic Benefits

greater savings would be projected due to mothers having fewer subsequent children, more mothers returning to work, and expected long-range reductions in delinquency and violent behavior in the children (Olds 1988).

The cost of the Hawaii Healthy Start program seems relatively low, about $2,000 per year per child (*Hawaii—Development at the Community Level,* unpublished), but I have seen no cost-benefit analysis for this program. However, the total annual cost for this program to cover all of Hawaii's at-risk families will be approximately $16 million. In contrast, Hawaii now spends $40 million a year on protective custody and foster care (Henkoff 1992).

A summary of the expected savings of such programs is provided in Figure 8–2. Again, I have combined the findings of more than one study (Barnett and Escobar 1990, Olds 1988) in order to develop this summary of economic benefits that could reasonably be expected.

EDUCATION FOR PARENTING FOR SCHOOL-AGE CHILDREN

Another context in which education for parenting can take place is in our schools. We feel that teaching the next generation about parenting while they are still children holds great promise. There has recently been an increased recognition of the potential benefits of an education for parenting curriculum in the schools (Zigler and Hall 1989). In 1986, the World Health Assembly advocated the teaching of parenting in public schools as one element in the primary prevention of neurological, mental, and psychosocial disorders (Earls and Eisenberg 1991).

Education For Parenting, a group of educators whose work began with the mental health (interdisciplinary) Education for Parenting program headed by H. Parens (see Chap. 7, this volume) and who were formerly affiliated with Germantown Friends School in Philadelphia, developed a curriculum for teaching parenting to school-age children. Their curriculum, *Learning About Parenting: Learning to Care,* is now in place in more than fifty schools in Philadelphia and across the country. Preliminary research with fifth grade students indicates that children who have been through this program are more knowledgeable about parenting. Furthermore, when presented with descriptions of common, difficult child-rearing situations, these children generate a greater number of nurturing solutions and fewer punitive ones (Raines, personal communication, 1992).

CONCLUSION

From my review of the literature, I am convinced that we know enough to establish comprehensive prevention and early intervention programs that are affordable and cost effective. I also feel certain that education for parenting has a crucial role to play in such programs. A significant body of research has demonstrated that these comprehensive programs, while not a panacea, can have a significant impact on many of our most urgent social problems, such as teenage pregnancy, low birth weight infants, child abuse and neglect, school dropout, welfare dependency, crime, and violence. The cost of these programs compares favorably to the cost of a year of public education. (For example, California now spends an estimated $4,500 per student each year, and New Jersey spends approximately $8,300 [Meyer 1992].) As a nation, we accept our responsibility to provide an education for our children. No less important is providing a foundation for love and care, self-esteem, the capacity to form loving relationships, a sense of competence, and good health, thus enabling children to learn in school and eventually become productive members of our society and helpful parents to their own children. In addition, I believe that the vast majority of our citizens would agree with this basic premise and would do what is necessary if they were aware that we could achieve such positive outcomes with a relatively small cost. When one considers the potentially vast savings—in both financial and human terms—the cost of these programs seems small indeed.

REFERENCES

Achenbach, T., Phares, V., Howell, C., et al. (1990). Seven-year outcome of the Vermont intervention program for low-birthweight infants. *Child Development* 61:1672–1681.

Ainsworth, M., Blehar, M., Waters, E., and Wall, S. (1978). *Patterns of Attachment.* Hillsdale, NJ: Lawrence Erlbaum.

Barnett, W. S., and Escobar, C. M. (1990). Economic cost and benefits of early intervention. In *Handbook of Early Childhood Intervention,* ed. S. Meisels and J. Shonkoff, pp. 560–582. New York: Cambridge University Press.

Berrueta-Clement, J. R., Schweinhart, L. J., Barnett, W. S., et al. (1984). *Changed Lives: The Effects of the Perry Preschool Program on Youths Through Age Nineteen.* Ypsilanti, MI: High/Scope.

Bowlby, J. (1969). *Attachment and Loss.* Vol. 1: *Attachment.* New York: Basic Books.

——— (1973). *Attachment and Loss.* Vol. 2: *Separation: Anxiety and Anger.* New York: Basic Books.

Breakey, G., and Pratt, B. (1991). Healthy growth for Hawaii's "Healthy Start": toward a systematic statewide approach to the prevention of child abuse and neglect. *Zero to Three* 11:16–22.

Children in Need: Investment Strategies for the Educationally Disadvantaged (1987). New York: Committee for Economic Development.

Earls, F., and Eisenberg, L. (1991). International perspectives in child psychiatry. In

Child and Adolescent Psychiatry: A Comprehensive Textbook, ed. M. Lewis, pp. 1189–1196. Baltimore: Williams & Wilkins.

Eisenberg, L. (1989). Public policy: risk factor or remedy? In *Prevention of Mental Disorders, Alcohol and Other Drug Use in Children and Adolescents,* ed. D. Shaffer, I. Phillips, and N. Enzer, pp. 125–149. (OSAP Prevention Monograph-2.) Rockville, MD: Office for Substance Abuse Prevention.

Elliot, L., Breakey, G., and Fox, L. (1991). *A Dance with Your Baby: A Guide to Infant Care Giving and Development—A Memory Book, Too!* Honolulu, HI: Hawaii Family Stress Center.

Erikson, E. (1968). *Identity: Youth and Crisis.* New York: W. W. Norton.

Freud, S. (1905). Three essays on the theory of sexuality. *Standard Edition* 7:123–243.

Fuddy, L. J. (n.d.). Lay home visitation in Hawaii: from demonstration to statewide system. Unpublished manuscript from Maternal and Child Health Branch of Department of Health, Honolulu, Hawaii. Received February 10, 1992.

Greenspan, S. I. (1981). *Psychopathology and Adaptation in Infancy and Early Childhood: Principles of Clinical Diagnosis and Preventive Intervention.* New York: International Universities Press.

______ (1982). Developmental morbidity in infants in multi-risk-factor families: clinical perspectives. *Public Health Reports* 97:16–23.

Hawaii—Development at the Community Level. (n.d.). Unpublished document from Maternal and Child Health Branch of Department of Health of Hawaii, Honolulu, Hawaii. Received February 10, 1992.

Henkoff, R. (1992). The kids are killing, dying, bleeding. *Fortune,* Special Report, Vol. 126, No. 3, August 10, pp. 62–69.

Mahler, M. S. (1988). *The Memoirs of Margaret S. Mahler,* ed. P. Stepansky. New York: Free Press/Macmillan.

Mahler, M. S., Pine, F., and Bergman, A. (1975). *The Psychological Birth of the Human Infant.* New York: Basic Books.

Meyer, M. (1992). Another lost generation: California schools are overflowing—and broke. *Newsweek,* May 4, pp. 70–72.

Olds, D. (1988). Prenatal/early infancy project. In *Fourteen Ounces of Prevention: Casebook for Practitioners,* ed. R. Price, E. Cowen, R. Lorion, and J. Ramos-McKay, pp. 9–23. Washington, DC: American Psychological Association.

Olds, D., and Henderson, C. (1989). The prevention of maltreatment. In *Child Maltreatment: Theory and Research on the Causes and Consequences of Child Abuse and Neglect,* ed. D. Cicchetti and V. Carlson, pp. 722–763. New York: Cambridge University Press.

Parens, H. (1979). *The Development of Aggression in Early Childhood.* New York: Jason Aronson.

Pfannensteil, J., and Seltzer, D. (1985). *Evaluation Report: New Parents as Teachers Project.* Jefferson City, MO: Missouri Department of Elementary and Secondary Education.

Provence, S., and Naylor, A. (1983). *Working with Disadvantaged Parents and Their Children: Scientific and Practice Issues.* New Haven, CT: Yale University Press.

Raines, B. (1992). Personal communication, April 20.

Rauh, V., Achenbach, T., Nurcombe, B., et al. (1988). Minimizing adverse effects of low birthweight: four-year results of an early intervention program. *Child Development* 59:544–553.

Sander, L. W. (1983). Polarity paradox, and the organizing process in development. In *Frontiers of Infant Psychiatry,* ed. J. Call, E. Galenson, and R. Tyson, pp. 333–346. New York: Basic Books.

——— (1985). Toward a logic of organization in psychobiological development. In *Biologic Response Styles: Clinical Implications,* ed. H. Klar and L. Siever, pp. 20–35. Washington, DC: American Psychiatric Press.

Schorr, L. B., and Schorr, D. (1988). *Within Our Reach: Breaking the Cycle of Disadvantage.* New York: Anchor/Doubleday.

Schweinhart, L., and Weikart, D. (1989). Early childhood experience and its effects. In *Primary Prevention and Promotion in the Schools,* vol. 12 in the series *Primary Prevention of Psychopathology,* ed. L. Bond and B. Compas, pp. 81–105. Newbury Park, CA: Sage.

Seitz, V., and Provence, S. (1990). Caregiver-focused models of early intervention. In *The Handbook of Early Childhood Intervention,* ed. S. Meisels and J. Shonkoff, pp. 400–427. New York: Cambridge University Press.

Seitz, V., Rosenbaum, L., and Apfel, N. (1985). Effects of family support intervention: a ten-year follow-up. *Child Development* 56:376–391.

Spitz, R. (1965). *The First Year of Life.* New York: International Universities Press.

Sroufe, A. L. (1982). The organization of emotional development. *Psychoanalytic Inquiry* 1:575–599.

Sroufe, A. L., and Fleeson, J. (1986). Attachment and the construction of relationships. In *The Nature and Development of Relationships,* ed. W. Hartup and Z. Rubin, pp. 51–71. Hillsdale, NJ: Lawrence Erlbaum.

Stern, D. N. (1977). *The First Relationship: Mother and Infant.* Cambridge, MA: Harvard University Press.

Vartuli, S., and Winter, M. (1989). Parents as first teachers. In *The Second Handbook on Parent Education,* ed. M. Fine, pp. 99–117. New York: Academic.

White, B. L. (1988). *Educating the Infant and Toddler.* Lexington, MA: Lexington/D. C. Heath.

Zigler, E., and Hall, N. (1989). Physical child abuse in America: past, present, and future. In *Child Maltreatment: Theory and Research on the Causes and Consequences of Child Abuse and Neglect,* ed. D. Cicchetti and V. Carlson, pp. 38–75. New York: Cambridge University Press.

9

DISCUSSION OF CHAPTERS BY DR. HENRI PARENS AND DR. WILLIAM SINGLETARY

John B. McDevitt, M.D.

Dr. Singletary reviews the literature on prevention (Chapter 8, this volume); Dr. Parens reviews his own work with prevention (Chapter 7, this volume). Parens begins by saying, "In my experience, prevention is not in the minds of most mental health professionals." This is indeed unfortunate since epidemiological studies have identified the important risk factors in childhood psychiatric, cognitive, and social disorders, and since, as the authors point out, prevention does work and is cost effective. Equally important, there is no other satisfactory solution to these disorders since, as a nation, we do not have the ability or the resources to provide effective treatment once they have become established. We are led to the unhappy conclusion that although prevention is necessary for mental health, prevention is not in the minds of most mental health professionals. This paradox says something important about us, our training, our institutions, and our society. In a recent book entitled *The Politics of Contentment,* John Kenneth Galbraith has painted a sad picture in which we—the contented majority—have turned our backs on the underclass as evidenced by the riots in Los Angeles and by the diminishing income and opportunities available to the underclass, particularly those who are disadvantaged and at risk. Thus, the gloomy picture for prevention is part of an even larger gloomy picture for the underclass. There are many possible types of help and prevention. Prevention programs will have to compete with other types of help such as Head Start and enriched school programs, which also must begin early in life and are cost effective.

Some aspects of preventive medicine are approved of and sought by the contented majority since they make sense, are believed to be advantageous (even for the underclass), and are relatively inexpensive. By contrast, prevention in mental health is not easily understood or proven to be effective in the long run, and is much more expensive. Prevention in mental health has to compete with many other forms of help for the underclass in terms of acceptability, political feasibility, reputed advantage, and cost effectiveness.

Not only do prevention and early intervention programs have to compete with other forms of assistance to the underclass, they have to compete with each other. They range from simple efforts to improve mental health in a short time period to comprehensive clinical approaches. For example, Dr. Singletary describes the $2,000-a-year cost of the Hawaiian Healthy Start program, the $5,000-a-year Perry Preschool Project, and the more comprehensive $8,000-a-year Yale Family Support Program. It becomes difficult to evaluate the relative efficacy of one program as opposed to another or the relative importance of different variables in any one program. These variables include continuity of competent personnel who, working as a team, address the mental health needs of both parent and child at an early age over a sufficient duration of time and with adequate frequency. When combined with basic support and health and educational services, these factors provide a comprehensive mix of services that can be individualized to the needs of each family and that establish the trust necessary for a preventive program to work.

Analyzing 162 preventive intervention efficacy studies,

White and Greenspan (1987) find compelling evidence of immediate, positive effect, but less compelling evidence of long-term impact, with the exception of the Perry Preschool Project. Most studies have not examined effects beyond three years after the completion of intervention. (An exception is the Yale Family Support Program.) White and Greenspan conclude that the most urgent need in the field is research that can inform practitioners and policymakers about the most effective forms of preventive intervention. They suggest that the specific nature of the interventive program being evaluated should in large part dictate the outcome measures that are selected and that the outcomes assessed should be indicated by the goals, activities, and underlying theory of the program. They detail the infant and maternal (environmental) variables that need to be assessed in order to plan interventions and stress that these variables must differ from the variables employed to assess outcome. They conclude that most existing reports have not been comprehensive or sufficiently clear in either intent or outcome measures. Therefore it is difficult to draw conclusions about the long-term effectiveness of any given approach or about the ingredients that would favor one type of intervention over another.

In presenting the background of their proposals Parens (Chapter 7, this volume) writes:

> In 1969 when we began our investigations into attempting to correlate qualitative aspects of the child-mother relationship with development of specific ego functions in the child, we did not know that some serendipitious findings would compel us into unanticipated areas of study and take us into prevention. Within two years of observing longitudinally mother-infant pairs in a group setting, meeting twice weekly with them for two-hour sessions, we discovered that unaware we had found a method for parenting education (pp. 124–125).

These two sentences, along with the promising follow-up study nineteen years later, are extremely informative. They tell us one of the reasons that prevention is in the minds of the authors if not in the minds of others, and they tell us something about how the authors view prevention and early intervention: at an early age with sufficient duration and frequency, and with emphasis on the mother–infant pair. Although the approach is educational, not psychotherapeutic, there are similarities with Fraiberg's psychotherapeutic work with infants with severe developmental disturbances. Most importantly, the baby is the *center* of the educational approach and the motivating factor in guiding the parents in caring for their child, just as the baby is the *center* of Fraiberg's therapy and provides the motivation for the parents to exhume the ghosts in the nursery. Parens makes this clear when he writes: "The focus of our attention in these groups is the children's behaviors, with a view toward talking about any issue pertinent to these behaviors found to be puzzling or troublesome to the mothers or to the children" (p. 125). Other similarities with Fraiberg's work are: frequency and duration of intervention, the early age of the children, and the training of the personnel—psychodynamically knowledgeable mental health professionals. The authors clearly provide us with the ingredients for a successful, comprehensive prevention and intervention program in both parenting education within the school system and in the work with groups of teenage mothers. Most important is the plan for a laboratory type curriculum. Not only is the baby the center of Fraiberg's therapy, the center of Mahler's research, and the center of education in Parens's mother–infant groups, he is also the center—or should we say the centerpiece—of the laboratory-type curriculum. Actual child–parent interactional activities in the classroom will interest and motivate the students, particularly the girls, to learn far more than lecture, discussion, or film.

The authors stress the difficulty in bringing the Oedipus complex to the classroom. Would it depend on how it is done? Would the use of myths, fairy tales, and literature be one way to present it in a manner that is acceptable? Why is it easier to discuss aggression during the preoedipal era, aggression that may be experienced later on as murderous, than the child's family romance, which later on is usually experienced as more loving than hating? Once it becomes genital, the loving presumably is more taboo because of its incestuous nature than is the hating.

Most exciting to me is the development of a comprehensive parenting program for students in the school who are already teen mothers, and most importantly, for their mothers: so often it is the grandmothers who raise the infants. The issues at stake in these programs are enormous, but I think that the time and effort will be more than worthwhile. I predict that the short- and long-term predictions Parens makes (Chapter 7, this volume, p. 145) will come true.

Both in Chapters 7 and 8 the term *research* is used. As far as I can gather, this term refers to the method of study of the outcome of the prevention and intervention approaches used. How do Parens and Singletary plan to research the effectiveness of the curriculum approach? At the end of Chapter 7 Parens assumes that both group comparative studies and individual case studies will be done. In addition to research that evaluates outcome, is this not a unique opportunity to study aspects of early development in this teen mother–infant population? This is an experiment in nature that might add to our reconstructive and prospective efforts through longitudinal studies to gain a closer and clearer picture of the origins of disturbances in development as well as a better understanding of how to prevent them. For example, in addition to teaching about rapprochement and object constancy, one might study the infants' particular development in this teen mother–child setting.

REFERENCES

Fraiberg, S. (1980). *Clinical Studies in Infant Mental Health: The First Year of Life.* New York: Basic Books.

Galbraith, J. K. (1992). *The Culture of Contentment.* Boston, MA: Houghton Mifflin.

Mahler, M. S., Pine, F., and Bergman, A. (1975). *The Psychological Birth of the Human Infant.* New York: Basic Books.

White, K. R., and Greenspan, S. I. (1987). *Basic Handbook of Child Psychiatry.* New York: Basic Books.

10

FOR PREVENTION: PROFESSIONAL TRAINING IN INFANT DEVELOPMENT AND PARENT EDUCATION

Elaine Frank, M.S.W. and Denise Rowe, B.A.

INTRODUCTION

The Early Child Development Training Program grew out of the work of Dr. Henri Parens and his colleagues at the Medical College of Pennsylvania (MCP) at Eastern Pennsylvania Psychiatric Institute (EPPI) in 1975. "The Early Child Development Program (ECDP) program was begun in 1970 to study the mother–child relationship and the effects of the availability and libidinal investment by the mother on the child's psychic development" (Parens 1974, p. 1). Parens began observing babies with their mothers to try to understand how aggression develops and operates in children and how it is dealt with by parents. He and his staff observed volunteer parents and their infants twice weekly. In return, staff tried to answer their child-rearing questions and help the mothers understand their children's behaviors.

Within six months the parents became enthusiastic and began to bring friends. Their children were puzzling to them and they appreciated answers to their questions and the staff's interest, which legitimized their own. One mother started a group that met in her home. The ECDP staff learned about this when she ran into difficulty and requested help, which was then given.

As the mothers became more interested in having their questions on parenting issues answered, the role of educator began to complement the role of observer. A group process emerged in which the instructor-observer focused the parents' attention on the children's behavior, involved them in observing their own and the other children, and explained the children's behavior in terms of psychodynamic theories of infant and child development. Although all the basic psychodynamic theories were used, Margaret Mahler's formulation of the separation-individuation process and Erikson's psychosocial theory proved especially easy to impart to the parents.

Learning about stranger reactions, separation anxiety, clinging, and tantrums helped even relatively uneducated parents to understand some of the contradictory and distressing aspects of personality development. As they understood more about normal developmental processes, they found that they could be more patient and flexible in their parenting. Gradually they felt better about themselves and their children. They appreciated the involvement of the child development experts, who helped them relax when things were normal and were there to spot trouble brewing.

The positive responses of the parents, many of whom continued to bring their children year after year, and the interest of staff and residents who came to take part in the baby watching, started the researchers thinking about the usefulness of an educational program based on this group process to help parents with child rearing. If parenting could be taught or improved by attendance in such a group, the method of experiential teaching might have potential use for prevention and early intervention.

Our experience revealed that certain truisms were not valid. For example, along with the data that (1) anyone who has a child can be a parent, it had been thought that (2) anyone who had training in child psychology could assist parents in the raising of their children. Neither is true. Truism 1 was shown to be unreliable as recent theories about early infancy and the impact of the parent–child relationship on personality development led to the realization that parents' interventions with their young children could be either growth promoting or growth disturbing. Many researchers have concluded that unrealistic expectations by parents about their child's behavior at different ages and stages of development tend to be associated with child neglect and abuse (Helfer and Kempe 1968).

BIFOCAL APPROACHES TO PREVENTION: PARENT EDUCATION AND STAFF DEVELOPMENT

We hoped that parent education could prove to be a direct path to prevention of behavior problems of early childhood as well as concomitant social problems such as learning disabilities, violence, child abuse, and juvenile delinquency. As these problems increased, especially in the cities, so did the search for remedies. The need for a program to train professionals in early child development and mental health became more and more pressing, for truism 2 was also found to be unreliable unless those trained in general child psychology were provided with developmental concepts.

Based on this experience, Parens, along with R. Hernit, designed a pilot program to teach mental health professionals child development theory, strategies for child rearing, and the implementation of the method they developed: Prevention/Early-Intervention Parent–Child Groups (Parens et al. 1974).

Those eligible for training included physicians (pediatricians, family practitioners, psychiatrists), psychologists, nurses, social workers, and teachers. In addition to learning the theoretical aspects of normal child development, trainees were taught observational skills and the methodology of group instruction.

The didactic seminars covered the physical and emotional development of children through age 6 and the parenting issues specific to these years. Lectures about physical development correlated emotional stages with biological maturational processes. Emotional development included Freud's oral, anal, and phallic stages and Erikson's stages of man. In addition, material was presented on:

1. Rene Spitz—the smiling response, stranger response and anxiety, separation anxiety, and anaclitic depression.
2. Margaret Mahler—the concept of symbiosis and the separation-individuation process.
3. Ego functions as related to mastery of traumatic events (e.g., hospitalizations, temporary separations, illness, and death).
4. Dependence in man—ambivalence and other conflicts related to dependency, between parents, or parents and child.
5. The libidinal, adaptive, defensive, and regressive aspects of play, fantasy, and related behavior.
6. The role of the father in the psychic development of the child.
7. The effects of parents' dynamics on their child's development.
8. The effects of social events on development.

Parenting issues discussed included limit setting and comforting, toilet training, temper tantrums, working mothers, sibling relations, adoption, divorce, foster care, sleep disturbances, reading the baby's cues, mother–child fit, and communication within the family.

In the first year the course continued for ten months, five hours per week, and was planned to include reading, the didactic seminars described above, participation in the laboratory group, and supervision. Supervision included discussion of trainees' observations as well as the methodology of group process. During a second year of training, group supervision of the trainee's actual work and experience in his or her own group provided an opportunity to enhance observational skills and to gain experience in leading the groups (Parens et al. 1974) (Hernit, unpublished).

As the training program grew, the work of other analytic theorists—including Anna Freud, Selma Fraiberg, Donald Winnicott, Stanley Greenspan, and Sally Provence—was incorporated into the curriculum. Also included were attachment and parenting researchers and teachers John Bowlby and Mary Ainsworth, and the work of pediatrician T. Berry Brazelton. The hands on or practicum part consisted of the students' observing the education for parenting group method, which includes parents, children, and instructors.

The pilot training program was originally designed to be an in-service model, drawing trainees from the hospital's staff who would be given the time to train and expected to apply the knowledge in their present positions and/or to begin new projects evolving from the training experience. It is noteworthy that this program began in 1975, before the current explosion of knowledge about infancy that led to the growing field of infant mental health and prevention. It was from this pilot project that the Infant Psychiatry Section at MCP/EPPI came into being.

EVOLUTION OF THE PROGRAM

While participating in the pilot training program, Rowe and Frank, social workers in the pediatric and child psychiatry departments, organized a mother–child group drawn from the clinic population at MCP. This provided the participants the double opportunity to engage in the parenting group process and assimilate observations and didactic material while providing a clinical intervention service for this population (Frank and Rowe 1981).

Work with this core group of parents and their children continued for four years in the general hospital; referrals came from hospital staff in the departments of pediatrics, obstetrics, and psychiatry. Eventually, the program became known throughout the local community, mothers from the area expressed interest in participating, and some local family practitioners and pediatricians began to refer their patients. Moderate fees were initiated and during the next four years, in addition to the original clinic population, families from higher socioeconomic groups, mainly self-referred, joined the program.

Our program was timely. It coincided with media coverage concerning new knowledge about babies and the increasing popularity of family life education. It was becoming stylish to learn about children and to work at improving parenting skills. Among mental health professionals, Mahler was becoming well known; her work, together with that of Brazelton, Greenspan, and Fraiberg, focused mental health practitioners' attention on earliest psychic development. Klaus and Kennell wrote about bonding, Bowlby wrote about attachment and loss, and Brazelton refined Spock for a new generation of parents. Now developmental psychologists studied attachment behavior in human babies and parents. At this very time frightening increases in the number of child abuse reports were filed. Cocaine became a major social problem, and child welfare workers were faced with a dismaying rise in family break-ups, which in some cases necessitated foster placement.

As remedies were sought it became evident that the earlier intervention was applied, the better the chances for effective results; and that prevention was even more essential because the emotional and societal damage was being passed on to the next generation. We needed new concepts and methods of prevention in family life, education, mental health, and social policy. The

National Institute for Mental Health (NIMH) created the National Center for Clinical Infant Programs. Cities, schools, social agencies, and mental health centers began to look for prevention programs.

EFFECTS OF THE PROGRAM

New skills in the use of parent education groups formed the foundation of prevention efforts by graduates of the Early Childhood Development training program. These graduates maintained the premise that if parents could assimilate the knowledge and principles of child development and child rearing they were taught in the parenting groups, and could thereby set limits with patience and sympathy, they would significantly increase the likelihood of raising healthy, competent adults to cope with the challenges of modern society. Hence, there was much enthusiasm for applying what had been learned to new endeavors in prevention.

Five years after the first training group graduated, MCP had five parent–infant groups led by the original trainees. In keeping with the original training objectives, the parent–infant groups were offered as an elective for junior medical students rotating through the psychiatry service, enabling them to observe infant and toddler behavior and mother–child interaction. The medical students enjoyed this rotation because they were able to observe parent–infant interaction with well babies. Some medical students or their spouses then attended the groups with their own infants.

Group leaders spent only a portion of their work time leading these groups but continued to meet for supervision and discussion. They were involved in planning an Infant Psychiatry Section within the department of psychiatry that would offer an evaluation and treatment program for families with children from birth to 4 years with mental health problems.

The training program graduated four more classes in the next years. These trainees came from other institutions and included nurses, educators, social workers, psychologists, and psychiatrists, who then returned to their facilities or began their own programs.

APPLICATIONS OF THE PARENT EDUCATION MODEL TO PRIMARY PREVENTION PROGRAMS

Described below is a variety of programs at both MCP/EPPI and other sites where expansion of the MCP groups could address some problems and needs of particular at-risk populations. These included child abuse, adolescent parents, and adoptive and foster families. As these programs were devised, we also applied our training by consulting with and facilitating groups for new parent education programs at other medical and social service agencies.

THE MEDICAL COLLEGE OF PENNSYLVANIA

The training program had prepared us to work with parents in need of knowledge about the emotional needs and cognitive development of their children. Membership on the hospital's Child Abuse Council familiarized us with the too frequent post-trauma efforts at treating abused children and their often extremely dysfunctional caregivers. Hospital staff worked hard to treat these children and tried to help their parents. They were all interested in finding ways to prevent the alarming rise in the incidence of abuse. We felt that attendance in a parent–child group could teach these parents to be more realistic about what to expect from normal toddlers and to cope with them less violently. Several families in which abuse had occurred were referred by family court of Philadelphia to attend a parent–child group.

Part of the group method is the explanation to the mothers of Mahler's separation-individuation process and its manifestations in the child's behaviors as the child experiences them. One goal is to help the mothers to "stand in their children's shoes," and even relive some of their own "childhood ghosts." Fraiberg's theory became integrated into the work as the mothers were encouraged to talk in the group about how they were parented (Fraiberg 1975). This was also done on an individual basis in parent–child psychotherapy in the Infant Psychiatry Section.

This intervention is especially critical where child abuse has occurred. We feel that if the mother can understand what troublesome behaviors are normal and learn to cope with them without violence, both she and the child will survive a critical period in their relationship. Although aggression is an important aspect of the mother–child relationship from very early on, the rapprochement subphase seems to be an especially dangerous one in mothers prone to abuse. At the age when toddlers normally become more aggressive, they also become more conflicted about closeness with their mothers. Intense maternal anger can be generated by the toddler's aggressive and ambivalent outbursts.

The most striking characteristic of parents who abuse is their unrealistic expectations of their children's behavior especially from birth to age 2. Steele and Pollock said that abusing parents "expect and demand a great deal from their infants and children. Not only is the demand for performance great but it is premature, clearly beyond the ability of the infant to comprehend what is wanted and to respond appropriately. Parents deal with the child as if he were much older than he really is" (1968, p. 95).

CASE ILLUSTRATION

Charles was hospitalized at 2 years 3 months with stomach pain due to possible liver damage after a beating by his mother. He had a bald spot on his head resulting from long hours lying in his crib during his first year. Child abuse charges were filed by the hospital and the child was discharged to the custody of his maternal great grandmother. When the case went to court, the hospital staff suggested referral to the parent–child group and the court made attendance mandatory if the mother wished to regain custody of Charles.

Charles's mother expected him to act older than his 2 years and not to cling to her—totally inimical to the nature of a lively toddler. A very positive characteristic of this mother was her expressed desire to keep Charles with her and to do a better job of parenting than had been done with her. She was also willing to put her embarrassment on the line and expose herself to us.

Charles's mother, a 20-year-old high school graduate with a childhood history of abuse by her parents had been left with her grandmother at age 9. One memory of her own abuse was of being tied to the potty at age 2½.

Although Charles's mother's pain was evident, at first she was sullen—she felt everyone was mad at her and suspicious of her ability to parent. Like many mothers who are new to a group she was afraid of what we would think of her child and her parenting. When they first came, Charles would look to his mother and she would look away. Left alone, his behavior became more disorganized and aggressive until he fell apart. Then his mother would move to punish. There was no interaction or communication other than those extremes.

Since Charles and mother had no means of expressing feelings or wishes, they were very limited in their relationship, with no range between command and hitting. Mother felt Charles should not need cuddling or reassurance from her and she pushed him away when he came to her lap.

One principle taught in the group is the importance of the mother's emotional availability. Two-year-olds can be enraging and parents need help in understanding how frightening it is for the toddler to feel out of control and then to worry that his mother may be helpless, which can be truly terrifying to both. Once the mother and child can converse about feelings, both have one of civilization's most important tools to prevent hostile aggression—diplomatic negotiation.

With Charles and mother's histories of violence and silence, they had little opportunity to obtain this experience. An example of their behavior follows: Charles asked mother for a snack. At first she didn't respond, which led to his insisting, whining, and eventually losing all control, rolling on the floor and crying. Her attempts to control him by yelling failed. She looked embarrassed, helpless, and finally asked us what to do besides hit him. We explained that 2-year-olds are often as anxious about their lack of control as they are stubborn. The child senses mother's fears and her inconsistent response causes him to become afraid too.

Mother was intrigued by the notion that Charles's angry loss of control might have an element of fear in it. She also liked the possibility that Charles might be able to understand her explanations now that he was learning to talk. She became more willing to try to talk to him when he misbehaved rather than to resort to yelling. Charles's willingness to listen and to talk back to her encouraged beginning dialogues.

A dilemma for the parent whose child has a tantrum is to know when to gratify the child and when to frustrate in the service of teaching self-control. A further dilemma for Charles's mother was that when upset he often sought comfort from her; she was then faced with whether or not to put her arms around the child she had just scolded. Comforting the scolded child can help him learn the lesson better, help him get better control of himself, and allow him to feel better about himself and his mother (Parens 1988). Since his mother had received so little comforting it was hard for her to believe that giving in would help Charles to learn to control himself. It took a lot of sympathy for her frustration from group leaders and other mothers before she felt given to enough to attempt to hold Charles and explain that we would have a snack soon but she wanted him to wait for the other kids.

By helping Charles's mother explain things to him just when he was developing language and to comfort as well as set limits, our intervention caused their interaction to become warmer and more gratifying. After a while we could see Charles catch himself when mother said that a snack would be served in a few more minutes. He would ask mother more questions about snack time but did not lose control.

The group provided a safe setting where Charles's needs were translated into terms that were understandable to his mother. Mother and child were encouraged to practice communicating using words and body language, skills that were new to both of them. The sympathetic concern of the leaders for mother's feelings gave her permission to express them, and allowed her to hear her child's feelings both spoken and unsaid. Our availability to mother enabled her to understand Charles's needs and respond to them, as well as to learn to limit him in a constructive way.

Although the parent education group is seen as preventive of a variety of parent–child interaction problems, it was felt that one or two abusive mothers could be integrated into a group, rather than attempting to form a group composed solely of abusers. Since abusive parents are usually in crisis the groups cannot accomplish the teaching of emotional development if too many members are in crisis at the same time.

Apart from the group, Charles's mother had individual treatment. The importance for an abusing parent to have one person to whom she can talk cannot be overemphasized. While efforts are made to treat abusive parents by short-term methods, we believe that the seriousness of this problem does not lend itself to short-term treatment; rather, intervention that is multifaceted and focuses on both parent and child, separately and together, is much more likely to succeed.

The mother's individual therapy helped her to make some peace with her own childhood experiences, and strengthened her resolve to raise Charles without physical punishment. At 9, he is a fourth grader who appears a bit older than his years, is doing well in school, and sometimes behaves like a big brother to his mother. She is finishing college and has a steady boyfriend. There have been no repeat episodes of abuse.

The common experience is that other mothers in these groups provide each other with support and encouragement. By learning to understand the emotional development and behavior of their children, the mothers become more empathic and sensitive to them. As the child responds to the more positive relationship, the mothers' self-esteem rises. Thus, mother and child have the opportunity for an increasingly mutually rewarding experience. Since much of what we discuss in the groups applies to all parents regardless of age, education, and socioeconomic status, mothers who are abusive or neglectful can benefit from this type of parent education in addition to individual therapeutic intervention.

ADOPTIVE PARENTS GROUP

Another special population in which a preventive approach was sought is the adoptive family. As research was conducted on early object relations, attention focused on the effects of infertility and adoption on parenting. In 1986 the Infant Psychiatry Section organized groups for adoptive families. Some specific issues for adoptive parents included reactions to infertility, loss of the hoped-for biological child, lack of pregnancy as a developmental phase, entitlement to parent, talking about adoption with their children, as well as the legal and psychological uncertainties in the adoption process. These issues may pose risks to the healthy emotional development of the mother–child relationship in this group and thereby to the adopted child (Frank and Rowe 1990).

There had been adoptive families in some of the earlier groups. In the new groups exclusively for adoptive families, particular concerns about growing up adopted could be explored by parents while their children were still small. We looked to the possibility of preventing problems thought to be linked to adoptive status such as excessive rebelliousness, low self-esteem, identity confusion, and depression. The goal was to prevent crises and to promote parental empathy by developing family relationships based on a strong emotional bond, mutual respect, and understanding of children's behavior. This excerpt from the authors' article in *Zero to Three* describes the launching of this program (Frank and Rowe 1990).

"We added a program specifically for adoptive families with the idea that they might be more comfortable in groups where pregnancy, delivery and nursing were not so much a part of group discussions, where they could describe the circumstances and express feelings about adoption. Until very recently there has been a dearth of post-adoption services. Many families are anxious or uncomfortable returning to an adoption agency with child development and parenting questions.

"Despite some preparation for parenting during the adoption process (usually limited to agency adoptions and not reaching participants in the growing number of independent adoptions), adoptive couples frequently have little knowledge about parenting or child development. They are often afraid to allow themselves to plan for child rearing, fearful that the adoption effort could be unsuccessful. Post placement parent education and knowledge about child development seemed critical for these families.

"If, in the early years, parents and child can forge a strong relationship and learn to communicate about emotional issues, adopted children are more likely to negotiate successfully the pains of learning about their particular adoption story. In group, parents could talk about child development and adoption issues, including infertility, birth parents, lack of medical information and 'telling.' Parents were also interested in how to respond to and educate family, friends and community about adoption.

"Adoptive family groups meet weekly for one and one half hours. Groups are also offered in the evenings for parents only. Before joining a group, each family meets individually with the leaders, and individual sessions are held at the end of the year. Parents can attend for up to three years (although one adoption group is entering its seventh year, with parents planning to continue until their children are grown!).

"By adding discussion about adoption to child development, parents explore their feelings and consider solutions to some of the questions about parenting and family life raised by the adoption situation. Topics discussed in the adoption groups during the children's second year illustrate common themes that emerge in all groups of this kind as well as those elaborations that are specific to adoption.

TOPICS AND THEMES IN GROUP DISCUSSION

"From the middle of the second year, the child's ambivalence, his urges toward autonomy, his separation anxiety, and faulty control of aggression—cause biological parents worry about their toddler's emotional stability. Adoptive parents worry more, wondering if problems from their child's unknown genetic past are surfacing, or whether troublesome behavior is due to an unknown aspect of the adoptive situation.

"If normal anger and aggression of young children take adoptive parents by surprise, parents also begin to fear about what will happen when their children become rebellious teens, or want to search for their birth parents. They feel guilty when they respond to their child's tantrums with anger of their own. Handling tantrums, setting limits and encouraging expression of feelings are on the group agenda now [Parens et al. 1987]. As leaders teach parents what to expect, parents are asked to express their concerns and to try out ways of handling both their feelings and their children. The original groups revealed that many biological parents are not prepared for these experiences either; adoptive parents often worry more than biological about the 'ghosts' of birth parents at this time.

"Between two and three years of age children have normal fears, especially of being left, lost, or not loved by parents because of bad behavior. These fears often coincide with parents thinking they should explain adoption to their children. The child's conscience is forming at this time, as is the sense of self as a separate person. He is really unable to entertain the idea of two sets of parents. Being 'given away' no matter what explanation is offered, is so frightening as to be disorganizing to the young ego.

"Although the content of fears may change as development proceeds in the early years, underlying themes of separation and abandonment remain constant. Parents are taught about these fears, and air their worries about them; they begin to think about how they will eventually explain the birth parents to their child.

"Through discussion, the leaders stress the importance of communication with one's child, especially about feelings and relationships. The strength and quality of the parent–child relationship is the most important factor in building self-esteem and contributes to a comfortable acceptance of adoption. Acceptance by parents of who their child is and how he or she became theirs has been correlated with a high level of self-confidence in adopted children (DiGiulio 1988, Hoopes and Stein 1985). As the child nears three, verbal communication becomes more and more a two way street. Child and parents have forged a sturdy partnership that will allow them to face the challenges of making sense of each child's specific adoption story.

"There is much controversy and discussion both within and outside of the adoption field about when and how to tell children about their birth parents. We feel that the 'when' should be related to the children's growing cognitive and emotional capacity to comprehend; and that the 'how' is the more important factor. It should include both an ongoing and episodic dialogue within the parent–child relationship as well as an atmosphere that encourages the sharing of feelings and ideas from the start of the child's life in the adoptive family.

BENEFITS OF POST ADOPTION GROUPS

"There are several benefits of a group that combines parent education with explorations of the adoption experience. The group provides an environment in which adoptive parents can work on issues in the presence of others who share them, and who are motivated to learn about their babies and their own new parental role.

"The experience of parenting, for which adoptive parents have waited so long, is exciting and rewarding. However, as with anything hard won, there is anxiety in the midst of satisfaction. Adoptive parents have been thrust into a situation for which they were over evaluated but under educated about the practicalities of parenting" (Frank and Rowe 1990, pp. 20–25).

EXPANDING THE DEMAND FOR PARENT EDUCATION

After a decade of applying the training program model to programs within MCP/EPPI, referral sources from city and community agencies requested parenting services for families of younger and younger children. There was a need for programs beyond the medical school setting. Graduates of the training program started groups at parenting resource centers at two community hospitals, a maternity hospital, and in an early childhood department at a local university.

Dr. Parens and staff began work on an extensive curriculum to be used in schools that would teach child development and parenting to children from grade school through high school (Parens et al. 1993). *Education for Parenting* was organized to offer prevention at the most basic level by starting in kindergarten to teach the responsibilities and skills needed for successful parenting.

SCHOOL-AGE PARENTS PROGRAM

In the late '70s there was increasing interest in Philadelphia and nationwide in the problems of adolescent pregnancy and child rearing. A grant was received from the Seybert Foundation in 1978 to provide parent education to the Philadelphia board of education's Services to School-Age Parents. This was a program for high school girls with babies who wanted to get their graduate equivalency diploma. Three days a week the girls attended high school classes at a center city site. They had to make their own baby-sitting arrangements because at that time no day care was available within the program. To enroll in the parent education class, the students were asked to come in once weekly outside of class time and to bring their babies with them.

The parent education method works most successfully when attendance is ongoing so that a relationship is established with the leaders. Girls who attended regularly gained knowledge of child development and parenting not provided in other aspects of their schooling. Because attendance was voluntary, this venture demonstrated the often unrealistic expectations adults have about adolescent responsibility. It is normal for adolescents to be ambivalent, rebellious, self-absorbed, and to vacillate between regressive childishness and budding maturity.

Separation-individuation theory has contributed greatly to our understanding of adolescent parenthood (Blos 1967). The leaders soon learned about the need for comprehensive programs for this age group with school, counseling, medical, and day-care services provided on site. Since this attempt, more encompassing model services have been underwritten and put in place to help adolescent parents. For example, at Children's Aid Society of Montgomery County, transportation service is provided to assist teens and their babies to attend a young mother's group where other parenting services are simultaneously available.

ABINGTON MEMORIAL HOSPITAL

As public interest grew in learning about parenting and the development of younger and younger children, some community hospitals added programs and services designed to involve young families in parent education. As consultants to Abington Memorial Hospital's Parenting Center, the authors facilitated a group that met behind a one-way mirror so that trainees from the staff of the child psychiatry department could observe the group. This was followed each week by supervisory meetings where the theory and method were taught in seminar style. The Parenting Center planned to provide observation opportunities of mother–child interaction to the family practice residents and to nurses and pediatricians on staff.

ADOPTION AND FOSTER CARE

In the area of foster care and adoption, the need for postplacement services for families has steadily increased; agencies wanted to respond to this need but had little preparation for dealing with early development and parenting issues. After Adoption & Parenting Services for Families[1] was founded to provide these services to families as well as to offer training and consultation to professionals in child welfare agencies.

Despite the fact that agencies are increasingly providing parenting services in the form of lectures and workshops, few have sufficient expertise and knowledge of early child development to competently bridge the gap between what researchers have learned and what parents know. Lectures and workshops that do not include observation and interaction of the children with their parents will not offer the depth and intensity of education that can be provided by well-trained professional instructors.

---

1. The authors are co-directors of this parenting service, located in Philadelphia, that provides parent–infant groups and child development and parenting consultation to professionals and institutions serving families with young children.

RESEARCH

Enthusiasm for prevention programs must be supported by evaluative research efforts. Parent satisfaction reports have been collected yearly, and Parens and colleagues have done a follow-up study on the participants of their earliest group (Parens 1993). We have been encouraged in our attempts to evaluate the effectiveness of the model by the recent analysis of research data that we collected in the 1980s. Preliminary results indicate that mothers attending this group showed more tolerance of their children's aggression, were able to foster independent activity, and exhibited more patience for their children's age-appropriate need for comforting and dependency behaviors.

Mothers who attended the group were compared to mothers in a matched control group who received no parent education. On some measures of the Maternal Attitude Scale (Cohler 1968), the control group mothers showed diminished ability to respond appropriately to their rapprochement-age children's appeals for closeness and to their normal temper tantrums and aggression toward their mothers. This research effort focuses on changes in the mothers and their parenting attitudes and behavior. Future projects will concentrate on differences in communication and expression of emotions in children who attend parent–child groups.

TRAINING OF PROFESSIONALS

Child care and day-care programs as well as nursery schools are accepting and creating programs for younger and younger children, sometimes as young as 6-weeks-old. However, undergraduate and graduate education in most fields still does not include in-depth study of the material on infancy, early childhood, and parenting available today. Even in psychology, psychiatry, and social work programs, education involving this knowledge is minimal. It is important for professionals working with young families to have at their disposal a thorough understanding of early emotional and cognitive development, as well as the methods and technique of imparting it, so that this information can be assimilated by parents and other students.

Teaching the developmental information and the group process method can best be accomplished in an in-service setting where trainees can have live or hands-on experience. It is important as well that the instructors be clinician–educators who have solid grounding in individual and group work. People running these programs should be sensitive to and respectful of individual and cultural differences, should know how to start where the parent–child pair is, and must have interviewing skills and ethical commitment to confidentiality; these are necessary foundations on which the training program is built.

In-service training is also given to paraprofessionals such as day-care workers as well as to various special interest groups of parents; however, training to lead parent–infant groups is reserved for those who already have certification in education, health care, mental health, and social services.

CONCLUSION

In the nearly two decades since the training program began, the notion of prevention in early childhood has rooted and taken hold in many forms and programs throughout the country. Infant mental health and parent education are recognized fields of service for educators and mental health practitioners.

We now know much more about the prevention of individual, family, and social problems and how important it is to begin prevention efforts as early as possible. The principal task in prevention is to transmit what is known about healthy child rearing to as many people as possible. Most parents are well-meaning and want to be good parents. While self-help, grass roots, and support groups have a place in sustaining and empowering parents, the need to train qualified professionals cannot be overestimated.

Well-trained professionals using the Prevention Early-Intervention Parent Education Model may produce a ripple effect on many kinds of families and social institutions. Scientific curiosity and a wish to observe the manner in which parent and child interact in the earliest years has led to the creation of a method of helping parents that can be taught and replicated. Widespread dissemination of child development information and parenting skills carried out by knowledgeable and supportive professionals can result in a vastly improved environment for growing up healthy in today's society.

REFERENCES

Blos, P. (1967). The second individuation process of adolescence. *Psychoanalytic Study of the Child* 22:162–186. New York: International Universities Press.

Cohler, B. (1968). Childrearing attitudes among mothers volunteering and revolunteering for a psychological study. *Psychological Reports* 23:603–612.

DiGiulio, J. T. (1988). Self-acceptance: a factor in the adoption process. *Child Welfare* 67:423–429.

Fraiberg, S., Adelson, E., and Shapiro, V. (1975). Ghosts in the nursery: a psychoanalytic approach to the problems of impaired infant–mother relationships. *American Journal of Child Psychiatry* 14:387–422.

Frank, E., and Rowe, D. (1981). Primary prevention: parent education, mother–infant groups in a general hospital setting. *Journal of Preventive Psychiatry* 1:169–178.

——— (1990). Preventive-intervention groups with adoptive parents and their babies: minimizing the risks to emotional development in the first three years. *Zero to Three* 10:19–25.

Helfer, R. E., and Kempe, C. H. (1968). *The Battered Child.* Chicago: University of Chicago Press.

Hernit, R. (1981). The early child development instructor's training program. (Revised). Unpublished manuscript.

Hoopes, J. L., and Stein, L. (1985). *Identity Formation in the Adopted Adolescent.* (The Delaware Valley Family Study.) New York: Child Welfare League of America.

Parens, H. (1974). Training program for leaders of prevention-intervention mother–child groups. Unpublished.

——— (1988). A psychoanalytic contribution toward rearing emotionally healthy children: education for parenting. In *New Concepts in Psychoanalytic Psychotherapy,* ed. J. M. Ross and W. A. Myers, pp. 120–138. Washington, DC: American Psychiatric Press.

Parens, H., Scattergood, E., Duff, A., and Singletary, W. (1993). Parenting education for emotional growth: a curriculum for students in grades K thru 12. (Work in progress).

Parens, H., Scattergood, E., Singletary, W., and Duff, A. (1987). *Aggression in Our Children: Coping with It Constructively.* Northvale, NJ: Jason Aronson.

Steele, B. F., and Pollock, C. B. (1968). A psychiatric study of parents who abuse infants and small children. In *The Battered Child,* 2nd ed., ed. R. E. Helfer and C. H. Kempe, p. 95. Chicago: University of Chicago Press.

11

EPILOGUE: WHERE ARE WE NOW? WHERE DO WE WANT TO GO? AND HOW WILL WE GET THERE?

Selma Kramer, M.D.

The symposium on which this book was based suggests that there is a tremendous need for prevention/early intervention projects. The major papers reported in this book address efforts at early intervention in troubled mother–infant pairs, most often with mothers who are chronologically young and emotionally younger, financially and educationally disadvantaged, and who often have, themselves, received inferior parenting often to the point of abuse. Only Henri Parens's projects and their outgrowths, as Frank and Rowe report, are truly preventative in nature; the others demonstrate valiant efforts at early intervention.

A recently published report on prevention by the American Academy of Child Psychiatry addresses many issues that are pertinent to this book. Shaffer and colleagues (1990) suggest that, in addition to the mother–infant pairs exemplified in this book, prevention measures should be made available to "children with psychiatrically ill parents; children with chronic physical illness; and children who have experienced a psychologically traumatizing event, such as a natural disaster, or who have witnessed the violent death of a loved one" (p. 11). Shaffer and his co-editors have markedly broadened the scope of mother-child pairs in need of prevention, and, I would add, early intervention.

This book presents prevention/early intervention efforts conducted by four scientific research centers as well as those summarized by Singletary, together describing very few programs. I hope that other centers will be motivated to carry out and report their prevention/early intervention measures.

Since the panel presentation of these papers at the 1992 Mahler Symposium, many psychologically traumatizing events have occurred, not the least of which are the Los Angeles riots with the unleashed aggression of hundreds of angry, frustrated, disadvantaged members of the underclass, followed a few months later by the natural, unleashed forces of hurricane Andrew. Each calamity caused devastating loss of personal property and integrity. Each imposed enormous strains on the entire family with terrible hopelessness.

WHERE DO WE FIT IN?

As dedicated as are psychiatrists and psychologists, our efforts are subject to the vagaries of governmental attitudes, changes in child-rearing practice, and changes in family structure. Basically, prevention efforts require active support of our leaders; programs require funding. Our lawmakers must stand up to the opposition of social and religious fundamentalist groups who oppose prevention and early intervention on the basis of interference with the rightful autonomy of the family. The fear of such interference is described with painful clarity in an editorial in the *Journal of the American Medical Association* (1992), which urges our government to take the stand already adopted by most other nations. According to Schaller and Nightingale, the United Nations General Assembly, in 1989, passed the International Convention on the Rights of the Child, thereby setting international standards for the treatment of children. These standards include the right: "to a name and a nationality; to protection and justice; to relief in time of disaster; to freedom from discrimination; to an adequate standard of living and medical care; to free speech; to an education; to a childhood with love, recreation, peace, and brotherhood; and, perhaps most important of all, the right to a future." Although this set of standards has been signed by 146 nations, *unfortunately, the United States has not done so.* Although the U.S. Senate and House of Representatives passed resolutions in 1990 urging President Bush to act on this convention, he did not do so (1992, p. 643; italics mine). Whether or not the current Clinton administration will do so remains to be seen.

Schaller and Nightingale, both pediatricians who show deep concern for the rights and health of children in these years of dreadful wars, civil unrest, and human rights abuses, remind us that in certain instances of unspeakable child abuse, as in the Nazi era, some physicians were active collaborators in promulgating the abuse upon children. They feel that

> Our actions as physicians should include recognizing situations where widespread violence is being directed against children or their families; documenting and understanding the physical, psychological, and developmental consequences of war or human rights abuses on children and seeking effective means of therapy for victims of such abuses; working to end the exploitation and degradation of children; addressing violations of medical and professional ethics such as collusion of health professionals in abuse of children and their families; and supporting our colleagues who seek to maintain ethical standards in difficult circumstances. [pp. 643–644]

Schaller and Nightingale believe that human rights atrocities occur in foreign countries all over the world. While some few of us are able to directly address these issues of violence abroad, I feel it is mandatory that we make efforts at prevention in our own country through wider scope issues and narrower scope issues, which are no less important.

SCOPES OF ACTION ON THE BEHALF OF CHILDREN

The wider scope issues include efforts to influence central and local governmental actions and processes, and social attitudes affecting civil rights, employment opportunities, physical and emotional security, availability of physical health care (including prenatal care for mothers and good medical care for their children), and mental health care. Employers are also within this wider scope; they now have considerable influence upon parents and children in terms of hiring practices, maternity leave, day-care facilities, and such. Law enforcement officers are also among this wider scope.

Churchill is said to have proclaimed: "There is no finer investment for any community than putting milk into babies." I feel that nourishment of our children requires much more than food: physical and mental health services, in particular, constitute Churchill's "finer investment," serving not only the current community but future generations as well.

Even in the narrow scope of influence, psychiatrists are not the first line of defense. Disturbed parents and children are referred to us by others; therefore, we must attempt to influence those in the front line. Parents, extended families, obstetricians, pediatricians, teachers, and churches have a much earlier and more immediate opportunity to recognize problems in parents and children. It behooves us to teach mental health concepts to these individuals and groups; to do so we must form a working alliance with them so that, as Parens did, we may positively influence parenting.

Shaffer and colleagues (1990) propose that "to launch a prevention program successfully, we must involve host organizations and individuals as full partners from the planning stage on and be aware of local sensitivities and experiences with similar interventions in the past" (p. 14).

Although our tasks seem formidable, we have among us colleagues who have worked toward prevention in ways other than the direct methods presented in this volume. Some have written and otherwise productively advised society. A shining example is Albert Solnit, who has influenced lawyers, courts, and lawmakers since the publication of *Beyond the Best Interests of the Child* (1973), co-authored by Anna Freud and Joseph Goldstein. No child custody decision has been made in the last twenty years without cognizance of this book, and the authors' later books *Before the Best Interests of the Child* and *In the Best Interests of the Child.* Solnit's latest book, *When Home is no Haven* (1992), declares that the child's interests must come first if he must be removed from the home for physical and mental safety. In addition, Dr. Solnit is now Commissioner of Mental Health for Connecticut. His impact will indeed be wide.

WHAT MAKES MAHLER'S CONCEPTS USEFUL IN PREVENTION/EARLY INTERVENTION

The research by Mahler and her co-workers enabled them to observe infants and their mothers and to conceptualize these observations in psychoanalytic developmental terms. Parens and his co-workers found it easy to translate Mahler's concepts into terms that would be understood and accepted by the mothers in their parenting projects. This understanding enabled them to grow as mothers and to be more empathic and comfortable interacting with and rearing their children. I was in the fortunate position of visiting Parens's original research group where I saw the great difference between the dread and antagonism of a mother new to the group toward her tantrum-prone two-year-old and the much more comfortable attitude of the mothers who had been in the education for parenting group for some time. Empowered by understanding, these latter mothers could contribute toward their children's autonomy and pride. When the mothers did not feel helpless, the children—although conflicted by their internal conflicting wishes and drives—did not feel helpless. The children seemed to feel emotionally protected and were not overrun by troublesome affects nor were they met with punitive hostility of the parents. I realize that Parens's original mother–child subjects were not of the same noxious background as were the pairs treated by Burland, Galenson, and possibly Egeland. Frank and Rowe's success in including some young, abusing mothers and their infants into the normal mother–child project might suggest a possible therapeutic milieu for some disturbed mother–child pairs.

WHY WERE SOME RESEARCH RESULTS DISAPPOINTING?

Burland and his co-workers attempted to help young, disadvantaged women become adequate mothers. His description of the mothers feeding themselves and not their infants certainly verifies Burland's contention that the mothers themselves had been poorly mothered. I would venture to propose that by constituting a place of oral gratification for these mothers, Burland's center may have given the mothers more than they or he realized. I contend that they became better mothers because of the experience. A five- or ten-year follow-up would reveal whether or not I am being overly optimistic.

Egeland's research raises some issues of concern. Were the mothers seen frequently enough and over a long enough period of time? Were those who attempted intervention well enough trained? Does Ainsworth's Strange Situation offer a sufficiently broad measure of the infants' growth as the result of intervention? As with Burland's project results, with follow-up after a period of years, I anticipate that more change occurred than was recognized.

The dramatic differences in Galenson's results with poor, disadvantaged mothers as compared to private-patient mothers demonstrate the importance of support systems for young mothers. I assume that the private patients had husbands who could provide emotional as well as financial sustenance, and that the babies had caregivers other than the mothers. I also guess that the women were older when they became mothers and were better educated in spite of their emotional disturbances that so adversely influenced the mother–infant relationship. Galenson's work displays the urgent need for external support (family, friends, society at large, professional help) when there is impoverishment of the ego of the young mother. All of the chapters attest to the need for longer therapeutic interventions.

Singletary's excellent discussion and summation of results of successful programs in other settings lead me to an item not mentioned specifically in any of the chapters: for whom does the mother get pregnant and what purpose does the baby serve for the mother and for others?

Many years ago I cooperated with pediatricians in a well-baby clinic at St. Christopher's Hospital for Children in Philadelphia. It appeared that many of the young, unmarried mothers wanted infants for one of the following two purposes: first, as a gift to the mother's own biological mother. In these cases the grandmother swept into the examining room proudly holding the infant. The young mother came in several steps behind her, carrying the diaper bags, each person's outer clothes, and more. The second use of the infant was as its mother's doll. These mothers brought in an extremely well-dressed infant who gave her great pleasure until the infant began to differentiate. Then the young mothers were discontented, even disconsolate, because their infants would not stay still, because they spat up and occasionally made a mess, or because they were "bad." More important than the messiness was the increasing manifestation of autonomy and normal hostility. At this point the young mother became pregnant again. The doll baby was showing independence and the young mother who so much wanted to be loved sought that love again. When a prevention program helped the young mothers to become more self-sufficient, less needy and hopeless, and to gain a better sense of self-worth and self-love, they did not need another self-sustaining pregnancy.

Prevention/early intervention measures must continue to be planned and tested. One hopes that their value will be accepted by the public at large, by government bodies, and by other sources of funding. The future of so many people is at stake.

REFERENCES

Schaller, J., and Nightingale, E. (1992). Editorial. *Journal of the American Medical Association* 268:642–644.

Shaffer, D., Phillips, I., Enzer, N., and Anthony, V. eds. (1990). *Prevention in Child and Adolescent Psychiatry: The Reduction of Risk for Mental Disorders.* Washington DC: American Academy of Child Psychiatry.

Solnit, A., Goldstein, J., and Freud, A. (1973). *Beyond the Best Interest of the Child.* New York: The Free Press.

Solnit, A., Nordhaus, B., and Lord, R. (1992). *When Home is No Haven.* New Haven, CT: Yale University Press.

INDEX